Finding Washington

Why America Needs to Rediscover the Virtues of Her Most Essential Founding Father

Richard Raines

ISBN 978-1-68570-376-9 (paperback)
ISBN 978-1-68570-378-3 (hardcover)
ISBN 978-1-68570-377-6 (digital)

Christian Faith Publishing
832 Park Avenue
Meadville, PA 16335
www.christianfaithpublishing.com

Printed in the United States of America

Acknowledgments

Finding Washington owes its existence to a lot of people. First, I wouldn't have written a single word without the love and encouragement of my wife, Jessica. Sweetheart, I love you more than life, and your passion for Jesus keeps our crazy family grounded. My kids were also quite involved, even if they didn't know it. Rebecca, Riley, Hannah, Reese, and Rhett…you had to endure boring diatribes from me when I managed to pull myself out of my office to talk about my book or whatever other soapbox I was on that day. I'm the first to admit that you guys have a mediocre dad, but your dad has awesome kids.

I'd also like to thank all the people that read the rough draft and offered feedback. Paul and Kim: you were the first to give feedback and nearly all your suggestions made the final draft. Thanks to my good friend Lance, a writer/editor/children's pastor extraordinaire, who was the first person to publish an article for me in *Christian Education Leadership Magazine*. Your opinion was the most coveted. A special thank you to Trisha, whose email is taped to the wall in my office for me to read when things got tough. Your constant encouragement means more than you'll ever know. And last, but certainly not the least, thank you, Karl, for your insight and enthusiasm but mostly for not judging me for wearing used shoes when I was a college student.

And thank you to you, the reader. The one thing I want more than anything in the world is for people to read my book. You've made that dream come true.

Preface

This book took a while to write. I spend quite a bit of time in the first chapter talking about the events which pushed me to write it, so I won't spoil it for you by retelling it here. However, I do think it's important to tell you that I've wanted to write a book my entire life, but I refused to force it out of some compulsion to simply get published. Although I think I've got a couple of books in me, this might be it, so I wanted to take my time. The preface to a book is supposed to be personal, so that's what I'll do...get personal. I'd like to do two things here. First, I want to tell you a personal story that some of you might think is weird. Second, I want to talk about us...Americans, and what we need to do to fix our mess.

I became a Christian when I was a teenager, and my dad was not particularly friendly toward Christianity. After he and my mother divorced, he got married and divorced two more times. When I turned eighteen, he met someone else, and they got married. Whoopee Doo. Another stepmom. I remember thinking, "I've seen this movie before." As it turned out, she was the real deal. She was a solid Christian and convinced my dad to start going to church with her, and he eventually became a Christian. My sweet stepmother Tena was standing in the room, calling out to Jesus when cancer took her husband and my dad from us.

Several years after my dad became a Christian and while I was attending college in Tennessee, my dad called and told me of a dream he had. He said that in his dream, he met an angel who took him to an old barn. When he looked in the barn, he saw a man, sitting alone at a typewriter, typing furiously. Confused, my dad asked who the man was, and the angel responded, "It's your son, Richard, doing what I've called him to do." I think about that dream a lot and, whether it was a real angelic visitation or the result of a bad burrito remains to be seen. However, I share that story with you to let you know that my dad's dream has significantly affected how I view the things I write. It's important to me that, you, the reader, understand that my compulsion to write is the result of a divine call that didn't come from my dad's dream but was confirmed by it. That's the first reason why I wrote this book. It's an extension of my faith, and I wish my dad was alive to hold his son's book in his hand.

Now, let's talk about the messes we've created for ourselves in this country. Things aren't good here at home. I think we are more divided now than we were at the start of the Civil War. The difference is that our current divisions aren't easily definable by state lines. The differences are ideological and spiritual, and I have a genuine fear that my kids will live through an all-out armed conflict between leftist anarchists and the rest of us. At some point, the government is going to demand that Americans give up their guns, and that will be the proverbial straw that breaks the camel's back. This really keeps me up at night, and it's the other reason I wrote this book. My prayer is that this book will ignite some genuine introspection, and that you, the reader, will embrace my notion that we desperately need a revival of the types of virtues George Washington displayed, and that you will take a minute and send me an email or two with your thoughts on how we can turn the tide.

I hope you enjoy the book. I wrote it for us.

Richard (richard@findingwashington.com)

CHAPTER I

Another Book about Washington?

A Year to Remember

Hey. Remember 2020? I'd like to forget too, but I can't, so I need your help. I'm trying to come up with a name for 2020. I believe we should give it an official title. I think the Chinese tradition of labeling each year could be instructive, but instead of something mystical like "The Year of the Dragon," we could come up with something more practical. Here are my ideas so far:

2020: The Year That Sucked. Perhaps this is too crass, but it certainly captures the essence of how most of us feel.

2020: The Year Introverts Will Remember as "The Golden Years." You know, because of social distancing.

2020: The Year Everyone on Twitter Agreed. Just kidding.

2020: The Most Peaceful Transition of Power in American History. Not really.

2020: The Year of Jumanji. If you haven't seen the movie, you won't get it. Keep reading.

2020: The Year of Sorrows. Kind of boring but accurate.

2020: The Year We'd All Like to Forget.

2020: The year we all thought was awful but held out hope that 2021 was going to be better, and then some dude in a Viking hat stormed the capital. I like this one, but I don't think it will fit on a hat. Before deciding on a slogan for 2020, perhaps we should conduct a brief review first.

I began writing this book on June 06, 2020. Although we were only at the halfway mark, we all knew that we were watching history unfold in horrifying slow motion. Many of us felt confident that, even with incomplete data in June, it was safe to label this year "crappy." Let's walk down memory lane together for a moment. Who remembers that a swarm of locusts descended on Africa in February and destroyed over 170 million acres of crops in Kenya and another 74 million acres in Ethiopia? What about the Australian wildfires and millions of acres of scorched land, destroyed homes, and the deaths of over 400 million animals? We were all shocked to receive the news that Kobe Bryant, his thirteen-year-old daughter, and seven other souls died in a helicopter crash on the way to a youth basketball game in Los Angeles but, unfortunately, this was only the beginning.

The year 2020 tried to ruin Ellen DeGeneres' life and career by making us think she was not nice, and a teenager named Charli developed a following of 100 million fans on TikTok for dancing and lip syncing, or whatever kids do on that app. I don't really know. I do know that seventy poor souls died in Indonesia because of floods and the Summer Olympics were postponed for a year. Oh, don't forget that Harry and Meghan left the royal family. I mean, I don't really care, but the media was obsessed with it. And if you think I'm being too hard on 2020, let's all take a minute and tip our hats to this year for sentencing Harvey Weinstein to prison, making sure Michael Bloomberg failed in his attempt to win the Democratic nomination for President and giving us Shakira and Jennifer Lopez at the Superbowl Halftime Show.

However, 2020's most notable achievement happened when someone in China attempted to make the world's best bowl of bat soup[1] and, in the process, unleashed a new virus, causing a global pandemic. Millions were infected worldwide, wearing a mask in

---

[1] Not true. It had nothing to do with soup. That was a poor attempt at humor. I floated several other ideas to my kids, but this is the one that stuck.

public became normal, there was a ridiculous shortage of toilet paper, and, hopefully, hugging nonfamily members was something that was gone for good. In the early days of the pandemic, we had to endure multiple public service announcements about how to properly wash hands. Many suggested that we should sing "Happy Birthday" twice while washing hands to ensure that we were washing for the appropriate amount of time. This became so ingrained in my mind that, when I would hear someone singing "Happy Birthday," I would rub my hands together. Living during a pandemic had also created new ways of working, which hadn't been terrible for less-than-social people like me.

In March of 2020, most of us had never heard of Zoom, but by the end of year, we were experts. Since I am in an industry where my interaction with customers is regulated by the FDA, Zoom *literally* saved my job. It allowed me and millions of others to work from home rather than collect unemployment. It's also worth noting that, as we all became more proficient with Zoom, introverts all over the world quickly discovered the secret of putting tape over their camera and then simply telling everyone it's not working, thereby avoiding even the appearance of social interaction.

I know it's probably too early in the book to start complaining, but I need to rant about what future generations will refer to as "The Great Toilet Paper Shortage of 2020." You already know what I'm going to say before I say it, but those of us that are eights on the Enneagram need to be heard. *It's a respiratory illness! It doesn't cause diarrhea!* True story: I spent three hours driving around Saint Augustine, Florida, looking for toilet paper at the beginning of the quarantine before coming home with two packs. I may have used a curse word or two to describe the present intelligence level of my fellow citizens. This cursed year also produced the death of one of the greatest entertainers of my generation: Kenny Rogers. He was the GOAT. If you're reading this and don't know who he is, I'm sorry that your parents didn't love you, I'm sorry you don't know all the words to "The Gambler" and "Coward of the County," and please go watch the movie *Six Pack*. It's awesome.

Overall, the Raines family was pretty fortunate in 2020 and, although I've suffered through periods of unemployment in the past, wasn't unemployed during the pandemic and tried to take advantage of working remote. In fact, most of this book was written from one of our most favorite vacation spots in the world: the Blue Ridge Mountains in North Georgia. Each morning during this week-long vacation, I would open my computer and look out across the mountains and marvel at the most beautiful sunrise I'd ever seen. My wife, Jessica, and our daughter Hannah would drive into town to get coffee and, on one morning in particular, I stared at the screen for what felt like hours, trying to find a way to communicate this next section.

Like you, I watched the video of George Floyd being detained and crying out for help, with cries that fell on deaf and unsympathetic ears. Like you, I watched George Floyd die. I didn't want to watch it but felt like I had to. The world needed to see it and not just hear about it. As I contemplate his death, I keep thinking that he died for nothing. He wasn't a martyr. He didn't die for a cause. He didn't stand his ground for a moral crusade and wasn't a warrior for any ideology. He went to a deli and purchased a pack of cigarettes with a $20 bill that the deli employee thought was counterfeit. The police arrived, and less than thirty minutes later, he was dead.

As expected, people began to gather to protest his death, which is a legitimate, legal, and time-honored American response to public issues. As many (including me) expected, they turned violent, and today, we're left with millions of dollars in property damage, more distrust, more anger, and no leadership; all the while, my heart hurts for George Floyd's family. My heart hurts for our country that needs healing. My heart hurts to see people profit from keeping us divided. My heart also hurts for Ahmaud Arbery's family. Arbery was chased down and shot to death while the man who shot him uttered the worst kind of racial slurs. The bottom line is that 2020 has been a year to remember, but not in a good way. I think I'll go with "The Year That Sucked."

Why Washington?

This might not matter to you, but this is the second version of this chapter. I had this chapter finished and was merely fine-tuning it before George Floyd's death. As the events surrounding his death began to unfold, I knew that I needed to write about it, so on the way to North Georgia, I said to Jessica in a rather defeated tone, "I think I need to rewrite the chapter." It's important, however, that you understand at least a little about what I included in my previous version because it's still relevant. I've been wanting to write this book for a while. I've been keeping notes and making outlines for over a year. The impetus, however, that caused me to open my computer and start typing, was an email I received from my pastor regarding the upcoming National Day of Prayer. The email wasn't anything out of the ordinary, and it wasn't actually written specifically to me. It was one of those "join me as we pray for our nation" emails to everyone in our church and an invitation to take the day seriously and pray that God would send revival to our nation. It got my attention enough that I thought it was finally time to start writing.

Why now? What was it about that email and the National Day of Prayer? I may be in the minority, but I'm one of those guys that prays for my country. I pray for our President and for Congress. I pray for our State leaders. I pray for our County Commissioners. I pray for my employer. I've been fortunate enough to lead people, and I know leading with the prayers of others is easier than leading without them. Maybe that's the impetus for this book, and maybe that's why I'm sitting here staring at my computer screen, taking double the amount of time it should take to finish this sentence...because I haven't been praying correctly.

I don't think I've been praying for the right things, and I'm fairly certain that praying once a year for our leaders isn't enough. As I continued to think about prayer, it dawned on me that George Washington had something to do with the first National Day of Prayer. I was wrong; he didn't, but I learned something else that tied all of this together and finally helped me understand why that when choosing a leader for The Continental Army it *had* to be Washington;

and when choosing the first president of the new republic it *had* to be Washington; and when looking for inspiration for this book, you guessed it, it *had* to be Washington.

No one knows for certain if this story is true, but the source appears to be reliable. Perhaps you've seen the portrait of General Washington kneeling in prayer in the snow next to his horse at Valley Forge. In the winter of 1777, The Continental Army was camped outside of Valley Forge, Pennsylvania, with little food and inadequate shelter. While it was not unusual for General Washington to visit local churches that were friendly to the rebel cause on Sundays, he was also known to find a place of solitude and pray. In his diary, the Reverend Nathaniel Snowden gives the following account of how one of his companions, a quaker named Isaac Potts, accidentally discovered Washington during one of his moments of solitary prayer. Snowden writes:

> I knew personally the celebrated Quaker Potts who saw Gen'l Washington, but I got it from the man myself, as follows: "I was riding with him (Mr. Potts) in Montgomery County, Penn'a near to the Valley Forge, where the army lay during the war of ye Revolution. Mr. Potts was a Senator in our State & a Whig. I told him I was agreeably surprised to find him a friend to his country as the Quakers were mostly Tories.
>
> He said, 'It was so and I was a rank Tory once, for I never believed that America c'd proceed against Great Britain whose fleets and armies covered the land and ocean, but something extraordinary converted me to the Good faith!'
>
> 'What was that?' I inquired.
>
> 'Do you see that woods, & that plain? It was about a quarter of a mile off from the place we were riding, as it happened.' 'There,' said he, 'laid the army of Washington. It was a most distress-

12

ing time of ye war, and all were for giving up the
Ship but that great and good man. In that woods
pointing to a close in view, I heard a plaintive
sound as, of a man at prayer. I tied my horse to a
sapling & went quietly into the woods & to my
astonishment I saw the great George Washington
on his knees alone, with his sword on one side
and his cocked hat on the other. He was at Prayer
to the God of the Armies, beseeching to inter-
pose with his Divine aid, as it was ye Crisis, &
the cause of the country, of humanity & of the
world.' 'Such a prayer I never heard from the lips
of man. I left him alone praying.'"[2]

At this point, I have no reason to doubt Reverend Snowden.
Maybe Potts saw Washington, and maybe he didn't. Perhaps it's
just another case of how Washington has become more myth than
man. However, I've read enough books about him to know that he
was contemplative, took his faith seriously (even if he wasn't devout
by some standards), and had integrity. Based on what we know of
Washington, Snowden's account rings true. As a student of American
history, Washington was, in his day, the indispensable man. He's the
one that kept the army together until the French could arrive and
help us defeat the British. He is the one that continuously inspired
the colonists to stay the course. It was Washington that pulled men
to Mount Vernon so that we could build a republic from a confed-
eracy, and it was Washington that laid his power down to prove that
America was better than a monarchy. It *had* to be Washington.

Finding Washington

I get it. This book has an unusual name, and even I struggle
with it. Each time I tell someone the name of this book, it takes five
minutes to explain what it's about. I'm pretty sure there's some indus-

---

[2] https://www.ushistory.org/valleyforge/washington/prayer.html

try protocol for naming books that would advise me to change it, but we're going with it. To explain why I'm writing this book and why I chose this title, we must go back to the presidential election campaign of 2016 because that's when I knew I had to write this book. *(Warning: I'm about to talk about politics, but that's not what this book is about. I'm only sharing the following story to illustrate what pushed me over the edge and solidified in my heart why I needed to write this book.)*

When the dust had finally settled on both the Democratic and Republican conventions in 2016, I had the most terrifying epiphany a voter could possibly have. I didn't have a candidate that really represented me in the election. I realized that in November, I was going to have to choose between the worst presidential candidate in my lifetime or the second worse presidential candidate in my lifetime. The most immoral presidential candidate in my lifetime, or the second most immoral presidential candidate in my lifetime. What a choice!

As an Evangelical Christian, I witnessed the American Evangelical Church undergo an identity crisis over which candidate to choose as some confused love of this country with the expression of their Christian faith. Others in the church were forced to use issues like abortion as a litmus test while still others simply chose to vote for the candidate that was less profane or sexist. It was the worst of times. Jessica and I eventually decided to vote for Donald Trump, but we did so based on a handful of political issues, with heavy hearts that we were casting our votes for someone that did not entirely represent us or our ideology.

The presidential election of 2020 was a similar circus. It was like the movie *Groundhog Day*, except this version wasn't funny. You know what, I would absolutely vote for Bill Murray at this point. "Dear God, please let someone nominate Bill Murray for President. Amen." Every time we have an election, the two major political parties hold primaries for local, state, and federal elections. Inevitably we're left with two choices while good people, who try to live their lives with some sense of morality, are forced to choose the lesser of two evils. Is that the fate of our nation? Is that the country I'm leaving my kids? When my grandfather was fighting in the Pacific theater in World War II, did he do it so I could choose between a potential traitor, who deleted emails and destroyed cell phones, or someone who thinks he can grab my daughters by the genitals if he wants to? Really? That's the greatest generation's legacy? We can do better. We are witnessing a leadership vacuum at every level in our country. We are so used to being betrayed by leaders that we're cynical about it. It disgusts me that the betrayal is so common that we've come to expect betrayal. Folks, we must do better. We *must*.

I've always wanted to write a book. Most narcissists do. I wrote a newspaper column back in the early 2000s that paid $10 per week. Jokes on them. I would have paid them $20 a week just to get my opinion published. While I was trying to decide whether to vote for the queen of all liars or the guy that couldn't be left alone with my daughters, I thought a lot about how incredible it would be if George Washington were still around. How amazing would it be if we had that type of leadership? I began reading everything I could get my hands on related to Washington and even listened to a handful of podcasts trying to get some inspiration for this book, but the opposite happened. I learned that at least 900 different books have been published about Washington, and there is an army of authors and historians alive today that know much more than me, and I became convinced that there wasn't really anything I could add to the conversation. However, as I considered Washington's life, I began thinking less about his accomplishments and more about the kind of man he was.

Before I continue, I need you to know something about me. I'm *extremely* sarcastic. It's my first language. I also like to make people laugh. It's how I hide the pain. This means I will say really sarcastic things and use humor to make my point many times throughout this book. However, these next statements about George Washington aren't sarcastic in any way or meant to be humorous at all. I mean them with all my heart. If he did not possess the virtues and characteristics that he possessed, we wouldn't have survived the first 100 years as a republic. If Washington had not been elected as the first President, I'm not certain the United States of America would exist today. If Washington had been killed in the Revolutionary War, it's unlikely that the United States Constitution would have ever been written.

As a matter of historical fact, Washington stands at the head of the founding of our nation. He wasn't just the head of the Continental Army. He didn't just cross the Delaware River on Christmas Day. He guided the formation of the republic and established *the* precedent for what it means to the chief executive of this country. He is, indeed, "The Father of our Nation."

There's no question that Washington was intelligent. I think it's fair to say that most of our founding fathers were extremely intelligent. He was a fierce competitor, a shrewd businessman, and a hard worker. He was a patriot that loved his country, an outdoorsman, and, like the rest of us, someone with personal flaws. He also possessed an internal moral compass that floated on a set of virtues, which set him apart from his peers. It was these virtues that caused the colonists to call on him for leadership time and again. It was these virtues that made him the only real choice for president.

As I reflect on the past two presidential elections, the deaths of Amaud Arbery and George Floyd, the ongoing riots and lack of leadership to deal with racial tension, and the leadership vacuum that exists on so many levels in our country, I know in my heart that the real solution, which is deeply embedded in my Christian faith, is for this country to experience a genuine spiritual awakening. However, I'll save that for another book and, instead, appeal more broadly to my fellow Americans by using the life and legacy of George Washington as an example of the kinds of virtues we need to rediscover to produce the kinds of leaders we so desperately need. That is why I have titled this book *Finding Washington*.

Over the next several pages, I want to lead us on a journey through the life of George Washington as he exhibits the characteristics that our leaders should embody...the characteristics which made him the kind of leader which inspired a nation and which inspired other nations to want to be free. Together, I want us to help our children find Washington in themselves. I want our boards of directors to find Washington to lead our corporations. I want our CEOs to find an army of Washingtons to serve as upper and middle management. I want our first-line managers to find the Washingtons among their employees so they can be promoted into leadership.

In the next round of elections, I want us to understand what the highest standard for American leadership is so that we won't compromise and, maybe, if God smiles on us, we can find President Washington again. *Finding Washington* isn't just about selecting leaders at the top. It's about developing and discovering those virtues that Washington exhibited that made him the ultimate example of American leadership. This isn't a self-help book for you to get better, although I hope you are inspired. This isn't a leadership book for businesses, although I hope business leaders are inspired. There are other really good books for those things. This is about us collectively. We need to understand Washington and the virtues he displayed and then *Find Washington* in ourselves, our peers, and those who lead us.

So let's go *Find Washington* together.

CHAPTER 2

Failure

Wet Powder and Dead Horses

Unless you're from Fayette County, Pennsylvania, this might be the one story you've never heard about George Washington. Modern-day Fayette County used to be part of the western frontier of the American colonies and was ground zero in the French and Indian War, which George Washington was probably responsible for starting when he was an officer in the British Army. After the war began, Robert Dinwiddie, the Lieutenant Governor of the Virginia Colony, sent Washington to Great Meadows (now Fayette County) to fortify and occupy Fort Necessity in anticipation of a French attack. When Washington arrived at the Fort, he noticed its state of disrepair and immediately began the task of fortification.

In addition to its state of disrepair, he also noticed that it was poorly stocked, and his men did not have proper equipment, so he wrote to Governor Dinwiddie, who promised to send him over seventy wagons of supplies from Winchester, Virginia. When the supplies arrived, only ten wagons came, which meant that Washington was still undersupplied. The other issue Washington dealt with during the summer of 1754 was men that were exceptionally undisciplined and suffering from low morale. Desertion was a constant problem, and historians believe that it was a deserter that informed the French of the location and condition of Fort Necessity.

As troops from other colonies started arriving, Washington began to explore the possibility of taking the fight to the French, so he ordered his men to move out. Along the way, he began trying to enlist surrounding Shawnee and Iroquois tribes to join him against the French, but they declined. Eventually, he abandoned his efforts to attack and, instead, returned to Fort Necessity and focused his attention on clearing brush from the battlefield, digging trenches, and making sure the troops had fresh supplies. As rain began falling on the morning of July 3, 1754, over two decades before Washington would ever think about commanding a rebel army of colonists, the French began to attack the British troops under Washington's command at Fort Necessity.

Although the fighting lasted all day, the Battle of Fort Necessity was over before it began. The incessant rain had filled the British trenches with water, which made it difficult to keep their gun powder dry, and the French, who Washington expected to attack in columns like a respectable European army, were hiding behind trees, stumps, and rocks, making it almost impossible for the British to target. Sometime after 8:00 p.m., the French stopped their attack and sent word that they would accept a British surrender, which could not have come at a better time for Washington.

One third of his men were dead or dying, many of the men had opened the rum and become intoxicated, the rain had ruined their ammunition, most of their weapons weren't even working anymore, and all the horses, along with the other livestock, had been killed in the battle. The French sent back a barely legible and wet note that said the British could surrender if they agreed to leave the Fort without destroying it and promise not to return for a year. Although history records that there were other conditions of the surrender that Washington didn't fully understand until later because he did not have an adequate translator that night, the important thing is that he and his remaining men were able to escape Fort Necessity with their lives.

There's no question that Washington took several lessons with him from Fort Necessity into the Revolutionary War. To start with, this was the first and last time he would surrender in a battle. The loss at Fort Necessity was humiliating. It certainly didn't help that, prior to the French attack, he bragged to Dinwiddie about how secure he and his men had made the fort. Secondly, it taught him that he always needed to have an escape route. One of the things that students of the Revolutionary War learn early into their studies is how surprisingly few battles Washington won. He was, however, a master at getting his troops out of the fight if things were not going their way.

When you get right down to it, you begin to think he spent the majority of the Revolutionary War running rather than fighting. Of course, that is a gross oversimplification, but the point is that Washington learned from his loss at Fort Necessity to make sure he had an exit plan for he and his troops. He also learned the value of keeping his men supplied. The history of the Revolutionary War is filled with examples of Washington constantly urging Congress to provide for the army. It may have been his biggest battle given that, even with his advocacy, the troops were sorely undersupplied for most of the war. It is scary to think how the war may have turned out had Washington not learned these lessons from Fort Necessity. What kind of leader do you suppose Washington would have been if he had been victorious at Fort Necessity? I guess we'll never know, but we certainly know what kind of leader he was after the loss.

WD40

I know what you're thinking. This is supposed to be a book about how we can mimic the virtues that George Washington embodied. You know, the good ones. Your mom got you this book for Christmas hoping that you would be inspired by George Washington's super-hero-esque qualities and start voting for the right political party for once in your life, and the first chapter is about him getting his butt kicked by the French...*by the French*...and then quitting. If you're thinking, *I'm not sure you know how this works, Richard*, it's ok. I promise you'll understand. Besides, everyone knows you can't get a refund on a used book, so you might as well keep reading.

Let's revisit Fort Necessity. Washington wasn't prepared. His men weren't prepared. He didn't have enough supplies. When he asked Dinwiddie for more supplies and was promised more, he didn't receive enough. His men weren't disciplined and many of them ran away, and at least one betrayed him. His equipment was subpar, the enemy fought dirty, and even the weather wouldn't cooperate. Like my dad used to say, he got his butt kicked six ways to Sunday. Like my kids say, it was an epic beatdown (I think they still say that).

The point here is that very early in Washington's career, he experienced failure and took those experiences and learned from them. When he was given the opportunity to lead men into battle again, he made sure those men were as well supplied as possible. We know from his personal correspondence that as soon as he took the reins of the Continental Army, he recognized that they were undersupplied and struggled to keep them supplied during the entire war. Yet he never wavered to be his troops' biggest advocate throughout the war. When faced with possible desertion and/or mutiny toward the end of the war, Washington used his experience from Fort Necessity to appeal to his officers' humanity, thereby snuffing out a potential rebellion from among his own troops.

I have a genuine question I want you to answer. When did we become so afraid of failure? Seriously? When did failing become such a bad thing? In our culture, failing is the worst possible thing that could happen to you, or so it seems. We've decided as a society to, instead, tell everyone that they are winners. It starts young, and it seems innocent enough. The eight-year-old T-Ball team goes 0-8 for the season because little Timmy crapped his pants last Saturday while playing second base, and Meghan's dad is living vicariously through his daughter by screaming at the top of his lungs as he coaches her from the bleachers, and half the team won't show up to practice on time. But you can bet your sweet butt cheeks that as soon as the last game is over, DeeDee's mom is collecting money so we can take the team to Chuck E. Cheese and give everyone a trophy and watch four-year-olds lick the floor. Am I wrong? Of course, I'm not wrong! Look, I don't get my underwear in a bunch over giving a memento to eight-year-olds for playing T-Ball, but do you see my point?

And here's what happens…those eight-year darlings grow into sixteen-year-old teens, who have been told that they're special since the day they were born, and that any failure was really someone else's fault. Now Liam and Emma are working at McDonald's, and as soon as the twenty-three-year-old night supervisor tells them they didn't clean the ice cream machine correctly and must reclean it, they are devastated and genuinely unnerved because, instead of their accomplishments being lauded, their failures have been highlighted. What started out as an innocent way to make sure kids got a trophy and a little positive reinforcement has, unfortunately, turned into a problem for the generation that will be putting us into retirement homes. And we see this everywhere.

When my oldest daughter was ten, she played church league basketball. I almost lost my mind when I found out they didn't keep score. I literally didn't understand why. Isn't that the point of the competition? To determine a winner? I was told it was so the loser wouldn't feel bad. *Shut the front door!* I don't even know how to respond to that. Am I the only person who thinks that's stupid? Although I've seen hundreds of dumb things in my life—and remember, I have two teenagers living at home, which means I see and hear dozens of new dumb things every day—watching my daughter play a season of basketball where no one kept score remains in the top ten dumbest things I've ever witnessed. Oh, and you can bet that there was at least one person in that gymnasium that kept score like it was his job and made sure to tell his ten-year-old daughter just how badly they dominated the other team. Now let's go to Chick-fil-a and get some of God's chicken to celebrate!

One of the places I see an aversion to failure the most is with the college students I teach. In addition to my full-time job, I also have a part-time job teaching world religions to college students. Each semester, I require my students to visit a religious service or ceremony outside of their religious tradition and then write a five hundred to seven-hundred-word essay about it. I am not exaggerating when I say that fifty percent of the students in the class do not know basic grammar, sentence structure, or spelling.

When I first began teaching, it was shocking. I can't begin to describe the simplicity of the errors. If I had to guess the average grade level proficiency of these students as it relates to grammar, I'd have to say somewhere around eighth grade. Did I tell you these are college students that had to have a minimum SAT or ACT score and a high school diploma for admission? During my first semester, I didn't know what to do when I started reading the essays. I contacted my department head, who also teaches world religions, and he suggested that, moving forward, I have the students submit a rough draft, but to get them through the current semester, treat the original submission like a rough draft and give them an opportunity to edit, which I did. Part of the problem is that these students coast through high school, and no one is telling them they can't write. We have an aversion to failure.

When did we forget that failure is part of the process? One of my favorite stories to illustrate this point is about a product you probably have somewhere in your home right now: WD40. In the 1950s Rocket Chemical Company in San Diego began working on a line of degreasers and solvents. One of their key inventions was a solvent that could displace water on moving parts. Since it took their engineers exactly forty formulations before it was perfected, they named the product, *WD (Water Displacement) 40 (fortieth formulation)*. This means that these chemists had to fail at least thirty-nine times in their pursuit of this formula. I can imagine Norm Larsen, the chief technician behind the project, kissing his wife on the cheek saying, "I've done it honey! WD28 is going to make us rich!"

The truth of the matter is, these chemists understood that the very nature of scientific research is that you almost never succeed on the first try, but, rather, you build on your failures. The inventors of WD40 most likely did not consider WD12, WD25, or WD38 failures at all. Instead, these were necessary steps towards success. I remember when my son Rhett was first learning to play baseball. It took him forever to learn to throw the ball straight, no matter how close I would get to him. No joke…that kid would look me in the face and throw the ball twenty yards to my left. Every time. In his moments of frustration, I would remind him that at one time, the greatest baseball players that ever lived couldn't throw the ball straight. In order to be good at something, you must fail first. No one just picks the baseball up and throws it as straight as they want, as far as they want, and as fast as they want the first time they throw it. Failure, it seems, is a part of success. That's why you don't have a can of WD25 under your kitchen sink.

Finding Washington

So, you're telling me that we need to find people who have failed and put them in positions of leadership? Well, yes and no. Let me explain. First of all, what I am not saying is that we look for people with low moral standards, whose lives are defined by moral failures. That's not the kind of failures I'm talking about. I'm not talking about the people who routinely make bad decisions and are known for poor judgment. I'm talking about people who have a good reputation, work hard, treat others well but have failed at something, possibly something big in their life. I'm saying that we don't judge people like this for their one or two failures; we judge them by how they respond to their failures. We judge them by their total body of work, not just their failures. It is important to note that if the Continental Congress had judged Washington only by his successes, he never would have commanded the army, and there are very few of us that would even know his name.

I want you to understand that failures shouldn't necessarily disqualify good people from getting the chance to do great things. History is filled with men and women that were failures, but, when given another chance, rose to the occasion. Few of us that love history doubt the important role Winston Churchill played in the allied victory in Europe in World War II. Yet, prior to becoming prime minister, Churchill had lost so many elections that he was, essentially, an outcast in his own political party. Had these failures been held against him and had his party refused to see that he had real value in spite of his failures, it is very likely Great Britain would have fallen to the Nazis. There's very little doubt that if Winston Churchill lived in the United States today and entered an election with the reputation for failure he had prior to his election as prime minister, there's no way he would win anything. Defeat, it seems, disqualifies people for leadership in our current culture.

The point I'm trying to make here is that, if history has taught us anything at all, it is that failure should not automatically disqualify someone from being promoted into a role which gives them more responsibility. If we are to find the Washingtons among us and within us, we must not disqualify others or ourselves because of failures. We all fail. Failure is a part of the human condition. It's how we respond to it that matters. We need to find those that respond to failure with tenacity and the drive to move forward in spite of failure. We should look for those among us that are self-aware enough to learn from failure and who do not shy away from the reality that, even though it happened, that particular failure won't happen again.

Washington's failure at Fort Necessity defined him, but not in the way most people think. It shaped the way he prepared for war. It affected the way he disciplined his troops, mapped out potential escape routes for battles, supplied the front lines, and sized up his enemy. Washington's failure at Fort Necessity wasn't a small thing. Men died. Husbands did not go home to their wives, and children were left fatherless. It wasn't just a personal failure that only affected Washington. He failed hundreds of other people, and he took that failure into every battle with him for the rest of his career and never surrendered his forces again. The Washingtons we find to lead us won't be perfect. They will be men and women with failures under their belt. It's how they respond to those failures that will determine whether we let them lead us or not.

Even if you aren't a religious person, I think you will appreciate the following story, which comes to us from the New Testament. When Jesus was alive, he personally selected twelve men to accompany him around first century Israel, and we have come to refer to these men as Jesus's disciples. One of these men was a fisherman named Simon, whom Jesus renamed Peter. Peter was an interesting character who was very charismatic, often spoke his mind and more often stuck his foot in his mouth, and generally lived his life with a substantial amount of passion. If the Enneagram would have existed in the first century, I think Peter would have been a six. He, along with two other disciples, formed a sort of inner circle of disciples that were particularly close to Jesus and, because of Peter's penchant for speaking up, he is often at the center of many of Jesus's most famous discourses.

Matthew, one of Jesus's disciples and a tax collector for the Romans, wrote an account of Jesus's life called the Gospel of Matthew. Since he traveled with Jesus and knew Peter personally, he had insight into a couple of events that you might find interesting. On the night before Jesus was betrayed by another of his disciples, Peter was bragging that even if everyone abandoned Jesus, he never would. In response, Jesus told him that before the night was over, Peter would disown him three times and, as you can imagine, Peter, with all of the bravado he could muster, objected and doubled down on his loyalty. If you haven't guessed by now, by the time the roosters were crowing to announce the sunrise the next morning, Peter had indeed denied his friend three times. That's not even the crappy part. Everyone that heard his bravado also heard him deny. The only thing Jesus had ever done was love Peter. He even saved him from drowning once and, in Jesus's moment of need, Peter denied any affiliation with him. What a failure.

Another of Jesus's disciples, John, who wrote his own account of Jesus's life (the Gospel of John), also recorded Peter's denial, but he records another event. After Jesus has been resurrected, he sees Peter on the beach. I'm not going to lie—it's an awkward meeting. I'll spare you the details, but in that meeting, Jesus lets Peter know that, despite his monumental failure, he is promoting him to something beyond his own capabilities. If you fast forward just a few weeks, Peter preaches the very first sermon of the Christian church, and three thousand people make a decision to become Christians. After that, Peter becomes one of the leaders in the Christian church and, eventually, dies as a martyr, refusing to deny Jesus to save his own life.

Look, you may be reading this and think Christianity and the New Testament are little more than children's fables, but I want you to focus on the story. We know that both Jesus and Peter were historical people that actually lived in the first century. We also know, as a historical fact, that Peter preached the first Christian sermon, and we know, as a historical fact, that he was executed for his faith. As a member of Jesus's inner circle, he was a first-class failure. I can't imagine failing at a higher level than Peter's failure, but look at how he responded to his failure. He was humble, and he set aside his false bravado and grew up a little. He understood the magnitude of what it meant to be a disciple and, although he wasn't worthy, took the promotion, and now, Christianity has more adherents than any other religion on the planet.

We must stop disqualifying people for failure. We must stop letting political opponents crucify each other for every small failure. We must stop making job applicants think they have to be perfect and, therefore, lie on their resume. We have to focus more on how people respond to failure and accept that failing is as much a part of the journey as breathing oxygen. If we want to find Washington, then we have to accept that his defeat at Fort Necessity preceded victory at Yorktown the same way every victory in your life has been preceded by defeats.

CHAPTER 3

Whole Numbers

My Dear Patsy

Before we go any farther, let's deal with the one-thousand-pound elephant in the room. When I was growing up, we were told that, as a boy, George Washington's father gave him a shiny new hatchet. One day, the future president took his new hatchet out to the orchard and cut down a cherry tree. When the elder Washington discovered that a cherry tree had been cut down, he asked his son if he was the culprit, to which he replied, "Father, I cannot tell a lie. It was I who cut down the cherry tree," thus displaying his impeccable character, even from a young age. If you went to public school in the seventies, I hope you're sitting down because it's my sad duty to report that this story is a myth. The story was invented shortly after Washington's death by Mason Locke Weems, one of the many writers eager to publish an account of the late president's life, and it appears the author fabricated this and other stories for no other reason than to sell books.[3]

This unfortunate ruse for profit by Weems and others led to an almost deification of Washington among the populace, which, for the most part, has been undone by serious historians. Although the cherry tree story is a myth, Weems was not fabricating Washington's reputation for honesty. Rather, he was taking a well-known virtue

---

[3] https://www.mountvernon.org/library/digitalhistory/digital-encyclopedia/article/cherry-tree-myth/

about the late president and fabricating a larger-than-life myth about how he expressed that virtue as a six-year-old. Imagine if someone wrote Michael Jordan's biography after he died and reported that when was six years old, he was dunking the basketball from the free throw line. Absurd, right? Well, in the 1800s the American people thought Washington was the closest thing to a superhero they could imagine, and Weems exploited their affection for him, but that doesn't mean Washington did not possess some of the virtues Weems mythologized, and in the same way, lying about Jordan dunking the ball at age six doesn't mean he didn't really do it at the 1988 Slam Dunk Contest!

There are dozens of stories from Washington's life that I could share that could highlight this next virtue, and I had a really cool story ready to share that I'll save for later, but my wife Jessica gets all of the credit for this one. We're still on vacation in the North Georgia mountains and, while visiting a bookstore today, she picked up a book titled *Letters of a Nation: A Collection of Extraordinary American Letters*, which contains letters from famous Americans like Meriwether Lewis and William Clark to the Oto Indians, Walt Whitman to the Town of Santa Fe, John Adams to his wife Abigail, and George Washington to his wife Martha, whom he affectionately called "Patsy." In the summer of 1775, the Continental Congress met and made Washington Commander of the Continental Army, a position for which he refused payment. After his appointment, he writes the following letter to his wife Martha:

> "My Dearest: I am now set down to write to you on a subject which fills me with inexpressible concern, and this concern is greatly aggravated and increased, when I reflect upon the uneasiness I know it will give you. It has been determined in Congress, that the whole army raised for the defence of the American cause shall be put under my care, and that it is necessary for me to proceed immediately to Boston to take upon me the command of it.

You may believe me, my dear Patsy, when I assure you, in the most solemn manner, that, so far from seeking this appointment, I have used every endeavor in my power to avoid it, not only from my unwillingness to part with you and the family, but from consciousness of its being a trust too great for my capacity, and that I should enjoy more real happiness in one month with you at home, than I have the most distant prospect of finding abroad, if my stay were to be seven times seven years. But as it has been a kind of destiny, that has thrown me upon this service, I shall hope that my undertaking is designed to answer some good purpose. You might, and I suppose did perceive, from the tenor of my letters, that I was apprehensive I could not avoid this appointment, as I did not pretend to intimate when I should return. That was the case. It was utterly out of my power to refuse this appointment, without exposing my character to such censures, as would have reflected dishonor upon myself, and given pain to my friends. This, I am sure, could not, and ought not, to be pleasing to you, and must have lessened me considerably in my own esteem, I shall rely, therefore, confidently on that Providence, which has heretofore preserved and been bountiful to me..."[4]

The Uniform

There's quite a bit of historical information we could unpack from this letter, and this reveals a lot about Washington we don't often get from the history books. When I initially planned to write

---

[4] .Andrew Carroll, Ed., *Letters of a Nation: A Collection of Extraordinary American Letters* (Kodanasha America: New York, 1997), 56–57.

this chapter, it was supposed to be about honesty, but once I really sat down and thought about it, I realized it was about so much more than that. This chapter is not just about telling the truth, which is what honesty is; it's about integrity, which, if you *really* read Washington's letter to Martha, sticks out like a hatchet in a cherry tree.

Before we talk about the letter, let's set the stage a little. In the summer of 1774, Washington attended the Continental Congress but wasn't appointed to a single committee by Congressional leadership. Washington wasn't one to openly debate issues and was more of a quiet, behind the scenes kind of guy everyone could rely one to offer wise counsel. The next summer, the relationship with Great Britain was deteriorating rapidly, and Congress began to call on Washington to serve on committees that would benefit from his military experience.

It was during this summer, in 1775, that I believe Washington announced to his fellow colonists what his opinion was regarding how the colonies should respond to the Crown. Although other members of Congress had served in the British military, only George Washington made the decision to begin wearing the red and blue uniform he wore in the French and Indian war to each session of Congress. He did not issue a written statement, and he didn't make a speech from the floor. He simply made up his mind that he knew what needed to be done, that he was willing to put on a uniform to do what needed to be done, and it was up to everyone else to make up their mind as well. That was Washington's way.

In his opinion, actions spoke louder than words, so he put on a uniform, letting Congress know that even if they weren't, he was ready to fight...today. It's important that you understand what this meant. Any action against the Crown that even smelled like rebellion was treason. The penalty for treason was death, and Washington knew it. If the colonists were to lose the war, Washington would be hanged, Mount Vernon given to a rival general, and Martha thrown out on the street. Make no mistake, when George Washington walked into his first session of the Continental Congress, wearing his old uniform—he was heading down a road from which there would be no return. It would be as Patrick Henry said a few months earlier, "Liberty or death."

Once the Congress decided that an army needed to be formed, it was a no-brainer for them regarding who should lead it. He was the most experienced among them. He was wise. He was well-respected, and he was available. Heck, he was already wearing a uniform! Of course, he agreed to do it, and his letter to "Patsy" reveals why. First, Washington believed that it was his destiny to lead the army. It may seem like he is contradicting himself when, on the one hand, he tells Martha that he tried to avoid his appointment while also referring to it as destiny, but I don't see it as a contradiction at all. It is entirely possible to know that one is destined for something while at the same time, wishing that you could avoid it. Secondly, he accepted his appointment because he was a man of integrity and knew that refusing to serve would bring "dishonor" upon both him and the people that put their faith in him. So let's talk about integrity.

Fundamental Concepts

I'm horrible at math. I know what you're thinking, "Yeah, me too." No, you don't understand. I failed geometry as a high school sophomore and had to take it again as a senior by attending classes at night. I did so poorly on the math portion of the SAT that, when I went to college, I had to take a remedial math class before they would let me take a class called "Fundamental Concepts of Mathematics." You read that correctly. I sucked so badly at math that they made me take a course designed to prepare me to take a class called "Fundamental Concepts." You would think that "Fundamental Concepts" would be the first class you take. You know…because it has *fundamental* in the name. In most cases, you would be right, unless the person you're talking about is an idiot. In that case, you would need a remedial class first. But wait, there's more! This story gets better!

My friend Kyle tutored me so I could pass my remedial class. That's right. I had to have a tutor for the class you take before you can learn the fundamentals. Kyle took time out of his busy life to sit with me for a few hours each week so I wouldn't fail a remedial math class. And you thought you were bad at math. Anyway, it was in this remedial class that I learned about integers, which is a fancy way of describing a number that isn't a fraction or doesn't have any decimals. It's a whole number. Since integer is the root word for integrity, it brings an entirely new meaning to the word. It means that a person with integrity is a whole person…not divided or constantly conflicted, not knowing which choice to make. A person with integrity knows what is right and does what is right.

I think Washington's letter to Martha is a great example of his integrity and a great example of what integrity is. Don't you see it? Let me explain. There are two things we know for certain. First, we know that Washington put on his uniform and attended the meetings of the Continental Congress. He was, essentially, volunteering for the job. There's no way anyone can convince me that he was surprised that he was asked to participate in an armed conflict against Great Britain when the Continental Congress finally decided to take that action. He may have been surprised that he was asked to take control of the army, but he was begging for a role by putting on his uniform every day. Wearing that red and blue officer's uniform to that meeting every day is the equivalent of a second grader jumping up and down in front of a teacher screaming, "Pick me! Pick me!" Secondly, we know from reading his letter to Martha that he didn't want the job. We know he didn't want it because he told Martha, in no uncertain terms, that he tried to avoid it.

You and I don't know each other, but I'm betting that you are beginning to doubt Washington's integrity and, perhaps, think that maybe he's downplaying things for Martha's sake. Perhaps this letter isn't a testament to his integrity. Maybe it's a testament to the fact that he played "my dear Patsy" for a fool. I don't think so. I think the opposite. I think Washington put on his uniform for reasons I've already discussed. He made up his mind that war was the way forward and wearing his uniform was his way of saying, "I'm ready to do my part." I think it fit his personality. He wasn't one to bloviate about his intentions or give political speeches. Anyone that knew Colonel Washington, as they all called him, would have known the meaning of his object lesson.

Secondly, I don't think he wanted the responsibility of leading the entire army. He had led men before, and he knew that, before this war ended, men would be dead, mothers would be without sons, and wives would be without husbands. As chief of the army, he would not just be responsible for fortifying a battlefront here or there, but for orchestrating the entire war, and he knew he was outmatched by his opponent. Simply stated, Colonel Washington knew his limits, and he sought to avoid putting himself in a position that would lead men to die.

I don't think he doubted his ability to lead. I don't think he lacked confidence. I simply think that he knew he lacked the traditional experience one would typically look for in a general, and, when he took an objective inventory of his resume, probably tried to convince Congress to choose another. The problem with that solution, and he was aware of this, is that there wasn't anyone else. He was the best they had. And this is why I think his letter to Martha speaks volumes about Washington's integrity. It's a personal letter to the person he loves and trusts the most, and he tells her things he won't tell anyone else. With this letter, we have a glimpse into the soul of Washington, and what we find is wholesomeness.

In this letter, he is saying that he has doubts and fears, but, in the end, he chooses the good of others over himself. He tells us that he can't bear to be away from his wife, but the country needs him. He tells us that he isn't the best choice, but his country has called him. He tells us that he wants them to find someone else, but his friends are relying on him. He says that rough times surely await him, but that he will rely on Providence, "which has heretofore preserved and been bountiful to me."[5]

Washington may be conflicted, but he is never torn. He may have had a difficult choice in front of him but is in no way divided or uncertain of what he should do. He is the epitome of what it means to be whole (integer), that is, he makes the right choice, even when it is hard. Scratch that. He makes the right choice, especially when it is hard, and that is the essence of integrity.

---

[5] Ibid., 57.

In the presence of all his fears and personal misgivings about his own abilities, the loneliness he would face being away from Martha, and the sheer weight of the position, Washington laid aside his own concerns and chose, instead, to put the needs of others ahead of himself. That fits any possible definition of integrity that I am aware of and gives us insight into what it means to have character, which we'll get to later.

Finding Washington

I'm not going to lie to you, integrity is hard to find these days in some circles. Don't get me wrong; it is still a valued commodity in our society, but I'm afraid that it is losing its value at an exponential rate. We must immediately begin selecting people with integrity to lead us and get rid of people who are in leadership who lack integrity. It's that important. I want to say that again so that you understand the urgency. We must begin *immediately*. What I'm about to say may be hard for you to hear, but I want you to promise me that you'll at least think about it. The next time you walk into the voting booth to select a mayor, county commissioner, or any other elected official, I want you to consider the integrity of the candidate first. Before any other consideration, consider integrity first. Ask yourself, "Which of these candidates expresses integrity at the highest level?" That means considering the candidate with the most integrity before political ideology. It's that important. Integrity is more important than political ideology.

Let me ask you a question. To which political party did John Adams belong? What about Thomas Jefferson? I'm betting that ninety-nine percent of you don't know the answer without looking it up. Adams was a Federalist, and Jefferson was a Democratic-Republican, and these two couldn't stand each other for a significant portion of their political life, but that's not how we see them. We see them as Founding Fathers. It's absurd to us to even consider that they belonged to opposing political parties. We're just glad they were elected because we knew what kind of men they were. I'm telling you; integrity matters more than whether your mayoral candidate wants to build a new city building or not. Integrity matters more than whether your county commissioner agrees with you on a zoning issue. Integrity matters more than a candidate's immigration policy. Perhaps now you are gaining insight into why the presidential election in 2016 was so difficult for me.

In regard to integrity in the workplace, it may be even more important than politics. I surveyed fbi.gov today for white-collar crimes that are being investigated or for which indictments or convictions have been issued and here are some of the headlines:[6]

- "Former President of First Mortgage Company Charged with 24 Counts of Financial Fraud"
- "Former Employee Admits to Stealing Nearly $10 Million"
- "Senior Executives at Major Chicken Producer Indicted on Antitrust Charges"
- "Nebraska Man Admits Stealing and Selling His Employer's Confidential Information"
- "Former Oil Executive Admits Role in False Payroll Scheme"

Here's the problem. It's not like corporations are holding open competitions for liars and thieves. It's that integrity isn't on the checklist anymore. Not at all. Maybe it's not fair to say *at all*, but you know what I mean. I think it starts innocently enough. A company wants to hire a sales force that will win in a competitive market. Corporate leadership instructs their managers to go and find candidates with a proven track record of success and don't hire anyone that hasn't finished in the top ten percent at their current job. Most of us would agree that this is a good strategy for finding qualified people. In this environment, finding salespeople that can win becomes the chief criteria, and no one is even thinking about integrity.

As managers build their teams, it is inevitable that, while most of the people that are hired are good people, a few of those people are the kind that have achieved their success by winning at any cost, and

---

[6] https://www.fbi.gov/investigate/white-collar-crime/news

36

they continue that trend in their new role. Their name is always at the top. They win their share of sales contests. They become models for other salespeople to emulate. As these employees grow with the company, some of them end up in management and some of them even end up in upper management or in C-Suite roles, and, from their perspective, winning by any means is a winning strategy. And suddenly, funds are embezzled, charges are filed for insider trading, or one day, a dozen women are telling their story of how they were sexually harassed by the same guy.

In the above example, it all started with simple oversight. No one purposefully omitted integrity. Some of the managers probably included integrity as a condition on their own, but most probably did not because they weren't thinking of it. And because the majority of the managers weren't thinking of it, a few bad apples got in and got promoted, and now, the entire company and, perhaps, an entire industry is suffering. We have to redesign the paradigm for how we build leaders, and it starts with choosing people who are asking to lead us and choosing people who may one day lead us, who display integrity. It also starts by making integrity a virtue we value again. If integrity becomes necessary for employment, necessary for advancement in employment, necessary for selection to serve in the public sector, then we can begin to slowly shift our culture in ways that will benefit this nation for generations.

I have a saying that I repeat to my kids all the time: "The right choice is almost always the hard choice." While we're going to seek out highly talented employees with high integrity, if we are forced to choose, we're going to have to start preferring integrity over other things we have traditionally valued in our employee candidates. In the same way, it's going to be really hard to choose integrity over political party, especially in these polarized times we live in. It's going to be hard for all of you, upper-level managers among us, to promote the person with integrity over the more talented person without integrity, but that's how we get this done.

I know some of you are going to disagree with me, and I want you to know that I'm teachable and will listen to you. But I want you, for this moment, to consider that Washington wasn't the most qualified, he wasn't the most talented, didn't have the best resume, and didn't even want to be Commander of the Continental Forces, yet, because of his integrity, he accepted the position and never wavered from his commitment to serve. Through seven long years of fighting, with few victories to show for it, Washington finally emerged victorious, and the rest is history. But we should never forget that, of all his commendable virtues, it was his integrity that set this nation on its course with destiny. It was his integrity that kept the army together. It was his integrity that gave the colonists and the Congress his trust, and it was his integrity, not his superior battle preparation, that kept him going when the war was almost lost. Likewise, it will either be our commitment to integrity that saves us or our abandonment of it that causes our demise. We must make the hard choice for integrity today, or we lose tomorrow.

CHAPTER 4

Pick a Virtue, Any Virtue

Dead Horses and Bullet Holes

Although I call Florida home, I've spent most of my life in Georgia, and I am, in every way, a Georgia boy. I am a ridiculously obnoxious Georgia Bulldog fan. I am an Atlanta Falcons fan, Atlanta Braves fan, and an Atlanta Hawks fan. If the state of Georgia had a professional ditch-digging team, I would buy a T-shirt and talk trash on social media about how Georgia ditch digging is superior to everyone else's ditch digging. As a red-blooded Georgian and life-long country music fan, I always try and support artists from my home state, and I always recommend to anyone traveling through Georgia that they attend former President Jimmy Carter's Sunday School class at Maranatha Baptist Church in Plains. If I find out that a movie was filmed in Georgia, I will watch it, and if I'm traveling and meet someone else from Georgia, I always feel an instant connection. So naturally, when former Georgia Congressman and Speaker of the House Newt Gingrich started a podcast (*Newt's World*), I *had* to listen and, lucky for us, his first episode was about George Washington and includes one of my favorite stories, which I want to share with you. Although my version of the story has facts that Speaker Gingrich's doesn't, I encourage you to check out his podcast anyway since he's not only a superior storyteller, but a fellow Georgian.

Not long after the debacle at Fort Necessity, the British realized that it was going to take a full-on military effort to deal with what they perceived to be French encroachment onto their land. It is important to remember that at this stage in the history of the American colonies, western Pennsylvania represented the frontier, and much of it was still inhabited by many Native American tribes, who were being forced farther west than they wanted to be due to European (particularly British colonial) expansion. Once General Edward Braddock arrived with his army, Washington was appointed as a colonial advisor, but it must be noted that mainland British aristocracy looked down their noses at the rough and uncultured American colonists.

Using his recent experience against the French at Fort Necessity as a backdrop, Washington tried to warn Braddock that the worst thing he could do would be to send his army in bright red uniforms into the Pennsylvania wilderness against a French and Indian force that didn't get the memo on proper European warfare, but Braddock refused to listen, so the redcoats marched west in a campaign to capture the French Fort Duquesne. On July 9, 1755, as the British troops worked to clear a road near the Monongahela River, the French and Indian forces attacked from the concealment of the forest. Seeing that his troops were disadvantaged, Braddock tried to call for a retreat but was shot and would die from his injuries a few days later.

This next part is very important and requires a bit of explanation. The average American male adult in 1755 was around five feet six inches tall compared to today's average height of five feet nine inches tall. George Washington was six feet two inches tall, which put him around eight inches taller than the average man. If George Washington lived today, he would be approximately six feet five inches tall.

As we return to our story, Washington saw that Braddock was wounded and immediately began to get him out of harm's way as the bulk of the British forces were fleeing the scene. Fortunately for Washington, rather than pursue, the French and Indians abandoned their attack and began trying to plunder the equipment that the British left behind. In the absence of any other commander, Washington took command, mounted his horse, and began to rally the troops for a counterattack. During the battle, Washington would have two horses shot from under him, and, by the day's end, he would discover four bullet holes in his coat but not a scratch on his body. After nearly twelve hours of fighting and commanding troops from horseback, Braddock commanded Washington to ride until he would find Colonel Thomas Dunbar and his men and order them to join the fight. Once Washington found Dunbar, he was too fatigued to return to the fight, and, at least for him, the Battle of Monongahela was over.

The Indian Prophecy

We're not done with this story yet. I told you it's my favorite George Washington story, and we're just getting to the good part, but let's chew on what has happened up to this point. Washington tried to tell Braddock what was going to happen, but, to no one's surprise, he didn't listen, and a lot of men died. However, when Braddock went down, George Washington, who was already the tallest guy in the forest, mounted a horse and added another two feet to his stature, thus making himself a very tempting target for the enemy, and took over the British counterattack. Not only did he command from his horse, but he fought from his horse. One of the things we know of George Washington is that he was an excellent horseman and was very agile. After the Revolutionary War, his officers would remark that they were surprised he survived because of the way he would fight with no regard for his own safety. You can imagine that in the months and years after this battle that Washington earned himself quite a reputation as a warrior, but it's important to note that it wasn't just his fellow colonists that took note of his heroics during the Battle of Monongahela. It was also his enemies.

As part of his service to the Crown in the French and Indian War, Washington was the recipient of land grants in the Ohio River Valley. In 1770, Washington traveled with his friend, Dr. James Craik, to view these lands and assess their value for agriculture or other uses. While in the area, Washington received an invitation to participate in a meeting with several Iroquois chiefs from the area. During his meeting with these chiefs, the conversation eventually turned to the Battle of Monongahela, and one chief in particular mentioned that he was present at the battle and remembered Washington because he and his men had tried so hard to kill him on that day but had failed. This chief then told Washington that a prophecy had been delivered about him based on his seeming invincibility that he would one day become the head of a powerful nation. The prophecy stated that "he will become the chief of nations, and a people yet unborn will hail him as the father of a mighty empire!"[7] Although Washington never wrote about the event, his friend Dr. Craik did. The story was made into a play in the 1800s but was eventually buried beneath the mountain of stories about George Washington's deeds as both general and president.

A Virtue Buffet

You know what, just pick a virtue from this story and run with it. You're not going to go wrong. We need all the virtues Washington displayed at Monongahela in all our leaders right now. That story alone could be the basis for a book, a movie based on the book, a Netflix teen drama with thirty-year-old actors who play teenagers with abs and substance abuse problems whose dads fight for Braddock, a podcast, an episode of *Walker, Texas Ranger*…you name it. That story has it all. I'm not even joking. I want you to sit somewhere quietly and read this story again, and I want you to think about everything Washington must have been thinking and feeling from the time Braddock told him to suck it up and get in formation to the time the enemy fired the first shot. You know that he knew it was coming. He was scanning the trees. He had been there at Fort Necessity, and he knew exactly what was going to happen, or at least he thought he did.

When the bullets started flying, everything that we knew Washington would eventually become came alive for a period of twelve hours, and what should have been a massacre and what began as a retreat became a real fight that had such an impact on the enemy

---

[7] https://www.mountvernon.org/library/digitalhistory/digital-encyclopedia/article/the-indian-prophecy/

that their religious leaders prophesied about Washington's greatness. That is the equivalent of an American soldier on D-Day, making such an impact on the Germans that they retreat back to their lines and write songs about him. Can you imagine? So with that in mind, I want you to put this book down for ten minutes before proceeding to the next section, and I want you to really think about what kind of moral virtues Washington must have possessed that drove his behavior during the Battle of Monongahela. And I want you to think about how our nation, your state, your local community, and your job or business can benefit from leaders that possess those virtues, and then I'll tell you what virtue really stuck out to me. See you in ten minutes.

Side Bar

I wish you and I could talk. I want so badly to hear your insights into what virtues you think Washington displayed most noticeably at Monongahela. You might find this odd, but I really want to hear from you. While you are welcome to email me about anything, I really want you to email me at richard@findingwashington.com your insights after reading this story. I can't wait to hear from you. Oh, by the way, please don't send hate mail. It's important that I think you like me.

Talking It Out

Before I unveil which of Washington's virtues that I think we should focus on from this story, I thought we should spend a little time talking out some of the other observations. The more I think about how Washington responded during the Battle of Monongahela, the more intrigued I am with him as a leader. In Newt's Gingrich's podcast, he mentions that the British aristocracy despised the colonists and considered them deficient in some ways. Regardless of Washington's accomplishments, the British aristocracy would have never accepted him among their ranks and would always have looked down on him. That was evident in the way Braddock brushed aside

Washington's battlefield intelligence regarding the enemy's method of attack. In spite of the fact that Washington had experienced the enemy's tactics firsthand at Fort Necessity, his lower station in life as a colonist disqualified him as far as Braddock was concerned. You have to wonder what Washington thought of this. He knows…*really* knows how the enemy will attack but can't do anything about it. So what does he do? He falls in line and does what is required of him, even when he is capable of providing more value.

I am also intrigued with how Washington initially responds when the French and Indians first attack. Historians tell us that Braddock is wounded almost immediately. In the pandemonium of the moment, Washington focuses on one task, which is to get Braddock to safety. At this point in the conflict, Washington was a junior officer, which is a stretch because he wasn't technically in the British army. Rather, he was in the Virginia militia. He even had a different color uniform. His official title on this expedition is aide-de-camp, which is a fancy way of saying he was Braddock's assistant. That means that his job was to do whatever Braddock needed him to do. So when the bullets were flying, Washington kept his eye on the ball, and, even though he would do a lot more before the day ended, he stayed true to his task and took care of Braddock. Clearly, the job Braddock assigned him was below his skill level, but he didn't complain. He did his job. He got Braddock out of harm's way, and, to a large extent, Braddock remained conscious enough to stay in command precisely because of Washington's quick thinking.

Then something else happened. Braddock looked around, and it was just he and Washington. As far as I know, the other officers had retreated or at least they weren't close enough for Braddock to issue orders. Washington was the closest thing to an officer that Braddock had, so he ordered Washington to mount a counteroffensive. That's all George Washington needed to hear. He climbed up on the first horse of the day and, rising nearly eight feet above the ground, found two hundred British soldiers to fight with him and, as he would learn firsthand fifteen years later while traveling with James Craik, strike fear in the heart of the enemy. They fired everything they had at him, but he kept fighting. They killed two of his horses, but he found a third. They shot through his coat but never touched him. He just kept fighting. I wonder what Braddock was thinking. I wonder to what extent he thought Washington was deficient now.

As he watched Washington float untouched above the fray, did he regret not listening to him? Did he marvel at the once-in-a-lifetime soldier he was witnessing command his troops? In the hours he had left to live, did he think, as the Iroquois did, that Washington had a destiny? I think the Braddock that sat injured on the ground near the Monongahela River in western Pennsylvania had a different philosophy about the American colonists than the Braddock that stepped onto American soil for the first time with his troops a few months earlier. Honestly, this entire story sounds made up, but I'm telling you, as far as I can tell from the historical record, everything I've just told you is accurate. And if you're wondering if there was one particular story about George Washington that pushed me to write this book, this is it.

Finding Washington

Five days. Five evening walks with Jessica, five days since returning home from vacation, and five days since I finished the previous paragraph. Would you like to know what I've been thinking about for five days? The Battle of Monongahela and the virtues George Washington displayed that day. More specifically, which one...and only one...to discuss with you. Which virtue is it that we need to identify as essential to leadership? Not just in current leaders but also in the next generation. The pressure is on because I can't mess this one up. This is *the* story about George Washington, and, in my opinion, this chapter and this story are the lynchpin that holds the rest of the chapters together. No pressure, right?

So Jessica and I are on a walk last night, and we're talking this out, and she mentions the similarities between Washington's behavior and the story of Joseph, which is found in the Old Testament book of Genesis. I'll let you read that story for yourself, but she was right. Let me explain. In the sixteenth century, Catholic monks in France began circulating a list of social guidelines that became very popular for directing social discourse across Europe and in the New World. By the time Washington was fourteen, he had copied these rules and created his own book, which is often referred to as *George Washington's 110 Rules of Civility*[8] and included rules such as Rule 40: "Strive not with your Superiors in argument, but always submit your judgment to others with modesty" and Rule 110, which read, "Labor to keep alive in your breast that little spark of celestial fire called conscience." As we survey Washington's life, we begin to see that, from a young age, he had a vision for the kind of man he wanted to become.

This next part is going to get a little theoretical, but I want you to bear with me. When I finished college, my first real job was training manager at a large industrial maintenance supply and hardware company in South Georgia. The owner hired me to work with his human resource manager to create a comprehensive training program for his staff of just over one hundred employees. The vision that I had for the training program revolved around the three core aspects of what I believe make up the essence of any individual: *Knowing, Doing, and Being. Knowing* consists of all the stuff we know…our knowledge. All of us possess varying degrees of knowledge on a variety of subjects, ranging from novice to expert.

Doing consists of the ethical activity we engage in. It's also the lack of ethical activity we engage in. When we do not possess personal knowledge of someone and must make a moral judgment of them, we often judge them by what we are able to see them doing. I'll give you an example: I listen to *The Bobby Bones Show* every day. To my knowledge, it is the only national morning radio show not broadcast on satellite radio that plays country music. Bobby and his on-air cohosts are like family to me, just like they are to all his listeners. If you listen, you know what I mean.

I don't know Bobby. He and I have never met and, other than what he has revealed to me through his radio show, a couple of books he has written, and social media, I don't know the first thing about him except that he likes the Arkansas Razorbacks almost as much as I like the Georgia Bulldogs. However, almost every time I turn on my

---

[8] https://www.mountvernon.org/george-washington/rules-of-civility/1/

radio, this guy is doing something good for someone else. If he's not raising money for St. Jude's Children's Hospital, he is putting bags together to feed the homeless. When his cohost, Amy, was trying to adopt two children from Haiti, he took a trip to meet the kids by himself. He purchases athletic uniforms for his former high school, gives scholarships to graduating high school seniors, and volunteers with other musicians to serve people in hospitals by playing music. Based on these examples, which aren't a fraction of the good things he has either done or helped others do, I would make a moral judgment about him that his ethical activity (his "doing") qualifies him as a "good" person.

Finally, we're left with *Being*. This is about who we are on the inside. This is about who we are when the lights are off, and no one is watching. *Being* is about the person only our dog and God knows about. The *real* you. I think that when we survey Washington's life from the time he was a child until the moment the first shot was fired at Monongahela, we see that he was striving desperately to cultivate *Knowing* by learning all he could without the benefit of the education some of his revolutionary peers received. Through learning and rewriting the *110 Rules of Civility*, he was trying to learn what it meant to *do* the right thing so that he would be considered a good person, and, somewhere along the way, Washington developed an internal virtuous ethic (*Being*) that I can only describe as a type of servant leadership that instinctively guided him.

By "instinctively" I mean that this servant leadership virtue became so ingrained in him that it ceased to be something he had to think about and more of an instinct. Before going too far, I want to dispel the myth that Washington was completely selfless and was a type of Jesus or Buddha figure. We know that he was a shrewd businessman, and he was extremely ambitious, but that doesn't mean his commitment to the principles of servant leadership weren't really a part of his personal ethos. I am convinced that, when you get right down to it, the chief virtue that Washington displayed at Monongahela was servant leadership, which was fueled by this internal set of core values he had developed somewhere along the way and the reason Jessica made the connection between Washington and Joseph.

Here's why: He was right about how they would be attacked, and he knew he was right. It was a suicide mission. In addition, he went from being the guy in charge of troops at Fort Necessity to no real role at all as an aide-de-camp to Braddock. Yet what did Washington do? Did he demand his rights? Did he protest? Did he throw a tantrum because he didn't get his way? No. Rule 40, which he learned at age fourteen, says don't argue, so he didn't argue with his superior. He accepted his assignment, which was to assist Braddock. And when the bullets started flying, he didn't grab a rifle and start shooting. He assisted Braddock. He was aide-de-camp of the century! Although he knew he was capable of more, he chose, instead, to serve Braddock because that's the role he had been placed in. It wasn't the role he wanted, it wasn't the role he was best suited for, and it wasn't the role for which he had been trained, but it was the role those in authority had placed him in and he found purpose in service. And the rest is history.

Please don't miss what I just said. Washington found purpose in service, even when he had earned the right to be served.

How much more do I really need to say? It is imperative that we do the following things immediately: First, we teach our children the value of servant leadership. Starting today, let's all agree to make our children do something for someone else every single day until it's part of their DNA. Don't pay any attention to how much they complain. They don't know what we know, which is if they grow up to be selfish and don't understand the value of servant leadership, our country is doomed. Selfish people make awful husbands, wives, and parents. Selfish people are crappy employees and even crappier managers.

Secondly, if you own a business or are able to hire or promote people, learn to identify people who have a servant's heart and are willing to serve others above their own interests. I'm not saying we ask employees to sacrifice their families for the job—that's ridiculous. What I am saying is that if we place value on servant leadership as a qualification for employment, then candidates will begin to value servant leadership, which means institutions that produce candidates will place a value on servant leadership and, before long, we've created a country of servant leaders. And for goodness' sake, if at all possible, let's start picking servant leaders when we vote. Let's demand that the people who are supposed to serve us possess the heart of a servant. Let's make one of the qualifications for "public servant" be "servant." Is that too much to ask? I don't think so. I think if you're still reading this book, you agree with me.

Don't forget to email me.

CHAPTER 5

Bloody Footprints and Bayonets

The Land of No Left Turns

I've had more than a few jobs in my life. My dad and grandad owned and operated Raines Painting Contractors, and I began working for them when I was eleven years old. When my parents divorced, and my mother remarried, her husband had his own pulpwood operation, which means if I wasn't painting houses with my dad during the summer, I was in the woods piling timber for my stepdad. I oddly enjoyed working with my stepdad at first because it allowed me to spend my days in the woods, which is still my favorite pastime. But once the temperature begins to exceed one hundred degrees and the humidity rises above ninety percent, being outside in South Georgia isn't fun at all. When I graduated from high school in 1989, I decided that there were easier ways to starve to death than paint or work in the pulpwoods, so I packed everything I owned into my 1978 Chevrolet Luv truck and moved to Tallahassee, Florida, to be closer to my sister, who had a friend, who had an uncle, who was an electrical contractor, and I became an electrician's helper making $5 per hour. I was on my way to financial freedom!

In the late 80s, the construction industry in the area tanked, so I made the decision to enroll at Lee College, now Lee University, in Cleveland, Tennessee. After enrolling at Lee, I continued earning money from what I learned as an electrician by working part-time for the school but spent most of my college years working for

Ace Hardware, which helped me land my first post-college job as a training manager. Although I loved my job as a training manager, my salary was so low I had to supplement my income by selling life insurance after hours. With a growing family, I knew I needed to earn more, so I talked to some friends who were pharmaceutical sales representatives, and they all said the same thing.

It's a really good job, but getting into the industry is harder than getting into the CIA, and they were right. I am now a sixteen-year veteran of the industry, and, since most of the companies I have worked for through the years are headquartered in New Jersey, I have taken more than my fair share of trips to the Garden State. The last time I was in New Jersey for a training event, my company rented several vans for us to drive and assigned a driver for each. Unfortunately, I was the designated driver for our group. I say "unfortunately" because I hate driving in New Jersey. Did I tell you I'm from Georgia? There were more animals than people in the county I grew up in, and traffic wasn't really a problem. Like most of my friends, I started driving very young because there was very little traffic on the roads, and our parents thought it was safe. The only dangerous things we had to worry about on the road were log trucks and tractors.

I was unhappy about driving in New Jersey for two reasons: First, I like to pump my own gas. I dare you to try and pump your own gas in New Jersey. They will rip you a new one if they catch you even looking at the pump because it's illegal for you to pump your own gas there. Secondly, in many places, you can't make a left-hand turn. Instead of turning left, you are forced to follow a detour, which locals refer to as "jug handles." They don't exist at every intersection, but in many places, instead of allowing you to turn left, you have to, instead, turn right and make a really elaborate 180-degree U-turn via an off-ramp, which usually has a traffic light at the end of it. Hey, New Jersey. You know what you could also do? Install turning lanes, and put arrows on your traffic lights. That way, each intersection doesn't take up ten acres of additional land. I can't wait for the emails about the superiority of jug handles.

While you may think that the life of a traveling pharmaceutical representative is all fun and games, it's usually all classroom learning and then studying clinical trials in the hotel room after dinner each night. One night on this trip, we found ourselves with some free time, so I suggested that our study group grab some dinner. One of our coworkers was familiar with the area and suggested a Japanese steakhouse in Pennsylvania, not far from where we were staying. As we were pulling out of the hotel parking lot, he nonchalantly said, "We're going to be crossing a narrow bridge. Are you okay with that?" What kind of question is that? I've been driving since I was eleven.

I responded, "I'm okay with that. Are the narrow bridges up here different than narrow bridges in the southeastern United States?"

He said, "Well, this one's kind of different, but you should be fine."

Twenty minutes later, I hear from the back of the van, "You might want to pull your mirrors in." And then, ahead of me, I see the narrowest bridge ever built. Holy cow.

In a panic, I said, "Are you telling me cars drive over this thing every day?" I'm not making this up people...the bridge is 877 feet long and looks wide enough for one pickup truck, and cars are going both ways. Every car had their mirrors tucked in because, if not, they would either hit the bridge on one side or the cars coming the opposite direction on the other side.

So there I was, driving 2.5 miles per hour in a white fifteen-passenger enterprise rental van, sweat dripping off my forehead and gripping the steering wheel so tight my fingers were numb. Meanwhile, really patient, God-fearing people from New Jersey honked their horns at me for going so slow. That wasn't the worst part. I could barely enjoy watching our hibachi chef build his onion volcano because as soon as dinner was over, I had to drive back across that bridge.

The Perplexity of My Situation

There was, however, one cool thing about that bridge. It was the exact spot where Washington's army crossed the Delaware River on December 25, 1776, with 2,400 troops on his way to engage three Hessian regiments in the town of Trenton, New Jersey. Even if you

slept through eighth grade history, you probably remember something about this story, or at least you've seen the painting by Emanuel
Leutze of General Washington standing very regally at the front of a
small boat while others struggled to row through the icy waters of the
Delaware River. The painting is quite an American classic and captures the pride all Americans feel when thinking about the sacrifices
that were made to purchase our freedom during the Revolutionary
War. What you may not know is the full story of what happened in
the days leading up to the Battle of Trenton, what happened after
Washington's men crossed the river, and some of the specifics of the
actual battle that took place the next day. Over the next two chapters,
we will unpack this historic event.

As 1776 was coming to a close, Washington was faced with the
reality that the enlistments of most of his soldiers would be up by
the end of December. Even a quick scan of his letters to Congress
reveals that the single most visited topic of 1776 was his insistence
that Congress invest in a standing army with lengthy enlistments.
There was quite a bit of resistance in the Congress to appoint a standing army, so the compromise was to, instead, call up the militia of the
several states. This presented a challenge for Washington because he
couldn't affect recruitment or length of service.

As Americans are fully aware, New England winters are brutal,
so the British assumed that both sides would take a break from major
engagements until the spring, a strategy Washington was prepared
for as well, especially with an army of soldiers whose enlistment was
ending. However, he knew that if 1776 ended without something
good happening for the colonists, his hopes of raising an army in the
spring might be slim. By the end of November, here's where the war
effort stood for Washington: New York City had fallen to the British
in September, and in just the month of November, the Americans
had lost both Fort Washington and Fort Lee. Although Washington
was able to evacuate most of the supplies from Fort Lee, between the
two forts, he lost over 3,000 men in the surrender of Fort Washington

as well as "146 cannon, nearly 3,000 muskets, 400,000 cartridges, a number of tents, and quantities of valuable tools."[9]

While the General was writing to Congress to explain the recent losses, he was also busy requesting shoes and clothing for the soldiers. On December 17, he wrote, "The Cloathing of the Troops is a matter of infinite importance, and if it could be accomplished, would have a happy effect. Their distresses are extremely great, many of 'em being entirely naked and most so thinly clad as to be unfit for service."[10] During this same month, Washington unintentionally opened a letter from General Charles Lee, which was addressed to Colonel Joseph Reed, and discovered that his two officers had lost faith in him. In Lee's letter, he criticized Washington for possessing a "fatal indecision of mind which in war is a much great disqualification than stupidity."[11] After mistakenly reading the letter, Washington simply sent it to Colonel Reed with a note expressing his apologies for opening it.

We have the good fortune to look back in history and know the outcome. We don't feel the slightest bit of anxiety over Washington's predicament because we know that it all worked out in the end. However, if we could place ourselves in his shoes for a moment, we would realize that things looked quite grim. His troops were getting ready to be released from service and, let's be honest, if they're spending their days outside in December in New England with hardly any clothes, home is where they want to be the most. He's lost New York City, Fort Washington, and Fort Lee. Two of his officers have lost faith in him, and Congress is either deaf or too preoccupied with other matters to give him what he needs to fight back. But, thankfully, the American colonists didn't have just anyone leading them—they had George Washington.

Not unlike the letter he wrote to Martha, I uncovered a letter he wrote on December 18, 1776, to his brother, John Augustine

[9] Andrew Allison and Jay Parry, *The Real George Washington: Part One: George Washington: The Man Who United America (A History of His Life)* (National Center for Constitutional Studies, 2009), 199.

[10] https://oll.libertyfund.org/titles/washington-the-writings-of-george-washington-vol-v-1776-1777

[11] Allison and Parry, 200.

Washington. You should read it. In the letter, he discussed all his frustrations, including what he thought British General Howe planned to do next. And in a moment of brutal transparency, the hero of Monongahela said the following, "You can form no idea of the perplexity of my situation. No man, I believe, ever had a greater choice of difficulties, and less means to extricate himself from them."[12] The weight of the world had fallen on his shoulders. In some of his other letters, he wrote about how the people of New Jersey were abandoning the cause and falling in with the British, and he was afraid that the people of Pennsylvania would do the same if the British made it across the river. He was losing at every turn and, though he wanted to mount up and fight, didn't have the men or artillery to match the British. It had been less than six months since Thomas Jefferson wrote the Declaration of Independence, and now Washington was on the verge of losing it all.

As a novice historian, I loved that I was able to get a glimpse into Washington's true thoughts by reading his letter to his brother. It's nice to know that the superhero of Monongahela was a real person. However, real fears and apprehensions aren't the only things he revealed in this letter. The sentence from his letter to his brother that I quoted earlier is part of a two-sentence section and appears at the end, right before the conclusion. Here's the full section with the part I left out earlier:

> You can form no idea of the perplexity of my situation. No man, I believe, ever had a greater choice of difficulties, and less means to extricate himself from them. However, under a full persuasion of the justice of our cause, I cannot entertain an Idea, that it will finally sink, tho' it may remain for some time under a cloud.[13]

[12] https://oll.libertyfund.org/titles/washington-the-writings-of-george-washington-vol-v-1776-1777

[13] https://oll.libertyfund.org/titles/washington-the-writings-of-george-washington-vol-v-1776-1777

Since the English language has evolved significantly in the 244 years since Washington wrote that, let me translate: *You cannot imagine how horrible my situation is. No person has ever faced such difficult problems with so few ways to solve those problems. However, I am fully convinced that our cause is the right cause I cannot even entertain the idea that we will lose, even if things look dark.*

Good Pizza, a Pretty Dress, and the Universe

I'm not sure I would have been that optimistic. My tone would have been more along the lines of "It's been a good ride" and "We're praying for a miracle." In the worst of circumstances, when he was mentally exhausted and alone (even his officers were showing signs of disbelief), Washington did two things: he acknowledged that things were tough all over, and that, regardless of how grim things looked, he was fighting on the right side of history, and he couldn't imagine losing. Losing wasn't even an option even if losing seemed like the only option.

When you compare Washington's letter to his brother to his more official correspondences, he doesn't reveal this type of transparency. He's very official and focuses his letters on the business at hand, making sure Congress knows about troop movements or requesting supplies. That's why this is such a big deal to me. His remarks about his commitment to the cause and belief in their victory weren't made public, and he didn't distribute this statement to the troops. He said it to his brother, almost as if he were confessing it privately. In my opinion, this is how we know he really meant it. He really believed in what he was doing, and he really believed that, because he was on the right side of history, they would figure out a way to win. What Washington was displaying in that two-sentence paragraph that I want us to learn from today is the virtue of genuine conviction and a commitment to action based on those convictions.

Perhaps it would be prudent at this point to make sure we are all on the same page with my definition of conviction. When we say someone has convictions, we generally mean that a person has strongly held beliefs about something, but I'm still afraid that definition isn't clear because we have a habit of overusing hyperbole to make a point. An example is the use of the word "awesome." If we eat pizza that is really good, we might say, "This pizza is awesome." If my wife comes out of the bedroom wearing a red evening gown, I might say, "Honey, you look awesome!" If I peer through a telescope at the night sky and see all the planets and the vastness of the universe I might say, "The universe is awesome!"

Do you see the problem? I don't think good pizza, my wife in a beautiful dress, and the vastness of the universe all qualify as awesome, at least not in the same way. In fact, if I had to pick only one of those things and strictly apply the definition of awesome (to be filled with amazement), I would choose my wife in a beautiful dress (you didn't think I was dumb enough to say otherwise, did you?). So, when I say that Washington had convictions, I mean the kind that he was willing to lose everything over. I mean the kind that he thought were so righteous and just that there was no way God was not on his side and, therefore, no possible way he could lose this war.

Finding Washington

As the history of the Revolutionary War would soon reveal, Washington's second-in-command, General Charles Lee, the same General Lee that betrayed him to Colonel Reed, had been ordered by Washington to march the troops under his command to Washington's location to support him against an impending attack by the British General Lord Cornwallis. As Washington's letter's reveal, Lee never comes. It turns out that Lee was jealous of Washington and thought himself a superior tactician. Many historians believe that Lee was purposefully disobeying Washington's orders, hoping that Washington would be either defeated or killed so that he would become commander in chief. Even those that think Lee had legitimate reasons for withholding his troops acknowledge that he was wrong to blatantly disobey the orders of his commanding officer.

Eventually, through gross negligence, Lee was captured by the British, released later during a prisoner exchange, and then court-martialed that year for his role in the retreat at the Battle of Monmouth, near modern-day Freehold Township, New Jersey. Lee was, in almost every way, the opposite of Washington. Instead of being driven by his convictions, Lee was driven by pure ambition. Instead of setting his pride aside like Washington did at Monongahela, Lee chose to put the entire war effort at risk for his own personal advancement. If Washington had not destroyed all the boats on the British side of the river, Lee's negligence would have meant the end of the war for the Americans. He was a narcissist of the worst kind, disrespectful of authority, and petulant. He was, it seems, the anti-Washington, and it showed.

We need to be very careful that we do not glorify the negative virtues Lee displayed, especially his obvious lack of convictions. What becomes of us if we lose our convictions in the things that are just? Maybe it's too late to ask that question because in many sectors, we already have. Perhaps we should, instead, ask what we are capable of becoming if we genuinely reaffirm deeply held convictions based on just causes and divine order. I think we need to believe in something again…something that unites us…that washes away what divides us and gives us purpose. We need convictions that are so deeply ingrained in our consciousness and imagination that we aren't tempted to give in to the fickle nature of the mob or the ever-shifting nature of public opinion.

What are your convictions? Do you have any deeply held beliefs that you would be willing to die over? I'm not talking about your family or your property. I'm talking about essential ideas or beliefs that shape who you are. I do, and I promise that if anyone ever reads this book, I'll write another one, and you'll know what those beliefs are. I can't tell you what your convictions should be. That's not how convictions work, but if you have deeply held beliefs that, if you died for them, God would greet you in eternity with a smile, then you're on the right track.

It is imperative that you and I…the people who make this country run, lead by example and live our lives from a set of deep-seated convictions. We've allowed the moral-less, conviction-less crowd to tell us what we should believe for too long. They have set the narrative and redefined terms. Up is down. Good is bad. Vulgarity is beautiful. Righteousness is oppression. Everything is tolerated except an intolerance to evil. General Washington faced a similar situation. The King of England said that the colonists were blessed to be a part of the glorious British Empire and were free as long as they acquiesced to the Crown. Washington held the conviction that he had been endowed by his creator with true freedom and believed his cause was just. As it turns out, he was right, and we are the beneficiaries of Washington's ability to stick to his convictions, regardless of the circumstances.

You may be thinking, "What do I do now?" Unfortunately, the best I can do here is provide hypothetical situations and try to stimulate your thinking, but I cannot define your convictions. I can only tell you to make sure your convictions are righteous rather than unrighteous. Remember, Hitler had convictions too. To those of you who already possess those convictions, I have a more direct admonition…stop simply believing, and start doing.

I'll give you a great example: My friend David and I are having a prolonged conversation right now about racism. Like all of us, he is sick of it. Like most of us, he can't point to any specific thing in his life that qualifies him as a racist, but he informed me today that being a nonracist wasn't enough for him anymore. He is under the conviction that he must take the position of an anti-racist, which requires action. As he wrestles with what that action should look like, he is seeking the advice of people farther along in the journey than he, but the point is that he is moving forward based on the conviction that he has a role to play to end racism, which certainly qualifies as a just cause.

I have another friend, Billy, who, along with his wife and daughters, fought hard to purchase a home so just a fraction of the large number of homeless high school students in our county could have a place to live. He was ultimately denied his request, but Billy and his family haven't stopped pursuing solutions for homelessness in our county.

And then there's Christine, who, as a school nurse, recognized several years ago that many of her elementary school students were not getting proper nutrition, and, although there was a charity that provided meals during the school year, these children often went hungry during the summer. So Christine started an initiative, contacted vendors, and recruited volunteers to help her pack hundreds of meals for children to eat when school is out for the summer. She followed her convictions.

Part of what it means to *find Washington* is to discover those convictions which place us on the right side of history and on God's side of issues, and then pursue action to affect change. That's how Washington changed history. That's how we will change it as well.

CHAPTER 6

Victory or Death

These Are the Times That Try Men Souls

We aren't done with Washington's decision to cross the Delaware River on Christmas and attack the Hessian troops at Trenton the next day. To clearly understand everything that happened that night, we need to do two things. First, let's recap: 1776 was coming to a close, and Washington was about to lose most of his army to expiring enlistments. He lost New York City, Fort Washington, and Fort Lee. He discovered that two of his officers had lost faith in him and were openly doubting his leadership, and one of those officers refused to send troops to reinforce Washington's vulnerable position. The men had no winter clothing, and many did not have shoes. Things weren't looking good, but Washington, a man with deep convictions, was dedicated to the cause. Secondly, we need to be properly introduced to Thomas Paine.

Born in England in 1737 to a quaker father and Anglican mother, Thomas Paine had a difficult time finding his way. He failed out of school before he was thirteen and, by age nineteen, had failed at learning to become a corset maker like his father. He tried becoming a deckhand on a ship, and when that didn't work out, he became an excise tax officer for the British Crown but was fired at least twice in a four-year span. In 1774, Paine met Benjamin Franklin in London, who persuaded him to move to Philadelphia. Once in America, Paine began his career as a journalist and eventually became the editor of *The Philadelphia Magazine*, where he excelled in the art of explaining many of the political ideals of the day to less educated `colonials.

On January 10, 1776, Paine published perhaps his most famous pamphlet *Common Sense*, which made the case for a representative form of government and argued for the natural rights of man, freedom of religion, and the need for the colonies to break away from the Crown. It was widely read by the colonists and was, perhaps, responsible for influencing more Americans to side with the revolutionary cause than any other document of that era. Thomas Paine, it seems, had found his calling. The popularity of this pamphlet also earned him the nickname *Common Sense*, which is what General Nathaniel Greene called him, even referring to him by that name in some of his official correspondences.

On December 19, 1776, as Washington plotted his daring move against the British and as his troops struggled to stay warm on the Pennsylvania side of the Delaware River, Thomas Paine began what would become a sixteen-essay treatise written over the next seven years he called *The American Crisis* which opened with:

> THESE are the times that try men's souls. The summer soldier and the sunshine patriot will, in this crisis, shrink from the service of his country but he that stands it NOW, deserves the love and thanks of man and woman. Tyranny, like hell, is not easily conquered; yet we have this consolation with us, that the harder the conflict, the more glorious the triumph. What we obtain, too cheap, we esteem too lightly: 'Tis dearness only that gives things its value. Heaven knows how to set a proper price upon its goods; and it would be strange indeed, if so celestial an article as Freedom should not be highly rated. Britain, with an army to enforce her tyranny, has declared, that she has a right (not only to TAX) but to "BIND us in ALL CASES WHATSOEVER," and if being bound

in that manner is not slavery, then is there such a thing as slavery upon earth. Even the expression is impious, for so unlimited a power can only belong to God.[14].

In a brilliant and poetic way, Paine had captured the heart of the revolutionary cause, and his words would be forever associated with Washington's most famous river crossing, and a victory which would inspire the colonists to stay the course in the fight for independence.

As Washington considered his battle plans and worked to secure enough boats to ferry 2,400 soldiers across the icy river, he worried about his soldiers' state of mind. Most were simply trying to stay warm and count the days until their enlistment ended, and they could go home. On December 23, 1776, as Washington was trying to prepare his troops for the upcoming raid on Trenton, he had the men form in ranks as the officers read Paine's first essay, which included these words:

> I call not upon a few, but all; not on THIS state or THAT truth but on EVERY state; up and help us; lay your shoulders to the wheel; better have too much force than too little, when so great an object is at stake. Let it be told to the future world, that in the depth of winter, when nothing but hope and virtue could survive, that the city and the country, alarmed at one common danger, come forth to meet and repulse it. Say not, that thousands are gone, turn out your tens of thousands; throw not the burhen of the day upon Providence, but "shew your faith by your works," that God may bless you. It matters not where you live, or what rank of life you hold, the evil or the blessing will reach you all. The far and the near,

---

[14] https://www.loc.gov/teachers/classroommaterials/presentationsandactivities/presentations/timeline/amrev/north/paine.html

11111111111111111111111111111111111111

the home counties and the back, the rich and the poor, shall suffer or rejoice alike.[15]

As the soldiers listened, it became apparent that Paine's words were having their desired effect on the men, and their posture began to change. Their hunched shoulders began to straighten, and the men made it clear to their general that they were, indeed, still in the fight and still committed to the cause. In response, Washington divided up his forces and began to prepare an exhausted group of colonials to go on the offensive against a well-rested, supplied, and formidable enemy.

Bloodstains in the Snow

It's no secret that we tend to romanticize the actions of soldiers in battle. In an effort to retell stories for future generations, we have a habit of inflating some of the aspects of these stories until, eventually, they become more myth than historical reality. To the best of my ability, I have endeavored to remain true to the historical record regarding George Washington's life and the events shared in this book, and the following story is no exception.

As Washington's men celebrated Christmas, they did so knowing that they would be embarking on a mission that night that would either be a nail in the coffin of their cause or a victory that would turn things around for the Americans. Whatever the case, they were ready. As the sun began to set, Washington marched his men to McKonkey's Ferry, the site of my narrow bridge story, and begin loading into boats operated by John Glover's famous Marbleheaders for the trip across the icy Delaware. Although Washington estimated that getting his troops across the river would take some time, he did not estimate that it would take eleven hours to ferry his troops across. Around 11:00 p.m., a winter storm set in on the area, and the wind, coupled with blinding snow and large ice formations that threat-

---

[15] https://www.loc.gov/teachers/classroommaterials/presentationsandactivities/ presentations/timeline/amrev/north/paine.html

ened to overturn the boats, significantly delayed the effort to cross. Meanwhile, his troops watched helplessly as the rain and snow wet their powder, making many of their rifles useless for the upcoming battle.

Once the men and artillery were safely across, the troops were organized into two divisions and began their ten-mile march to the town of Trenton, New Jersey, where up to 1,400 German Hessian soldiers guarded the town. Colonel Johann Rall, who commanded the Hessians at Trenton, was spending Christmas night at a house party, celebrating the holiday by playing cards with friends. A few hours before Washington had finished his trip across the river, a local Tory had spied the Continental Army's activity and sped to Trenton to get word to Rall. When the Tory arrived at the home where Rall was staying, stating that he had an urgent message for the colonel, Rall refused to see him. A combination of Christmas festivities and a howling storm outside had lulled Rall into thinking that, at least for this night, there was no chance of an American attack.

When the Tory spy was informed that Rall would not see him, he scribbled a message on paper and asked the host to give the urgent message to Rall. When Rall received the message, he stuck it in his pocket without reading and continued with the evening's celebration. Meanwhile, as the Continentals marched towards Trenton, the state of their muskets continued to decline. When news of this reached Washington, he informed his officers that the men should fix bayonets, for there was no going back now. The next day, when Major James Wilkinson was bringing his troops to Trenton to support Washington, he remarked that he could easily follow the route the Americans had taken by the bloodstains left in the snow by the soldiers who marched in bare feet.

Victory at Last

Around 8:00 a.m. on December 26, 1776, Washington's troops converged on Trenton, catching the Hessians completely by surprise. Rall rushed to organize his troops along the parallel King and Queen streets, but American artillery, under the command of Alexander

Hamilton, was waiting for them. Hamilton's men fired down at the Hessians, sending them into a full retreat as their cannons prepared to fire on the Americans. At that same time, a troop of Virginia militiamen, led by future President James Monroe, charged the Hessian artillery with bayonets fixed and captured the cannons. While most of the Continentals were fighting with bayonets, some were able to keep their powder dry enough to fire on the Hessians, killing Colonel Rall, who was found dead with a note in his pocket, warning of the attack.

In the chaos, there were some German-born soldiers among Washington's men that called out (in German) to the Hessians to surrender, resulting in a victory for the Americans. By the end of the battle, the Americans had killed or wounded 115 and taken 1,000 Hessians prisoner. Miraculously, the Americans did not lose a single soldier in the fighting, though two froze to death during the storm the night before. Although not considered a strategic victory, Washington's decision to attack Trenton did indeed turn the tide for the Americans. In response to his victory, Congress expanded Washington's war powers, authorizing him to raise and equip an additional sixteen regiments, including a system for promotions, having Tories arrested, and gathering supplies for the army.

Inspiration

At this point, there are a few things we need to remember about Washington. He was, as we have said, a man of few words. He was not inclined to give speeches and rarely spoke publicly unless it was necessary. Often, his silence was mistaken for brooding, but this was typically an observation made by those who did not know him. He was also aware that he was not as educated as some of the other Founding Fathers, which persuaded him to speak only when necessary even more. Although Washington loved his troops (he regularly tossed the medicine ball with them for exercise), he often allowed his officers to verbalize his wishes.

As he drew his battle plans for Trenton, Washington knew the sacrifices his men had made and were making, and he knew how increasingly despondent they were becoming. It wasn't in Washington's nature to give a locker room speech, but fortunately for him, Thomas Paine had written the ultimate locker room speech. Washington made the decision to have Paine's *Crisis* read to the troops, which proved to be the lynchpin in his plans for an attack. Without sufficient motivation...without helping the troops rediscover why they signed up to fight in the first place, not only did he risk losing the battle for Trenton, but the entire war effort might be lost. It's tough to put ourselves in Washington's shoes because we know how it worked out.

If you could, however, try and imagine his thought process as he considered the attack on Trenton. As long as he could get across the river undetected, the battle strategy was solid. He had crossed the river before and knew that it was possible, but the unknown element of his plan was whether his troops, who were just days away from going home, would fight. It was a real concern. We don't have any reason to think the troops would have mutinied, but men had already been deserting in high numbers, and it was likely that any talk of engaging the British would accelerate desertions. Additionally, he had to ask if they could fight. The men were without shoes and proper winter clothing, and they were at the point of starving due to a lack of food. Washington was afraid that simply giving the order to fight might not be enough.

His decision to have *Crisis* read to the troops, as we now know, was the perfect motivation. It wasn't the first time Washington had employed this strategy. On July 9, 1776, Washington had the Declaration of Independence read to his barely trained troops as they prepared for a defense of New York against 32,000 highly trained and rested British soldiers. Washington's virtue on display in these moments was his ability as a leader to inspire his troops to face a better-trained, better-supplied enemy in weather conditions, for which they didn't have proper clothes or shoes and face that enemy with determination and a belief in their cause. As a leader, Washington's ability to inspire his troops perhaps exceeded his capabilities as a military tactician, and there's little doubt that the American Revolution would have survived beyond the spring of 1777 had he not been such an inspiring leader.

Survey Says!

My dad, who had no use for politics, was a young teenager when John F. Kennedy was president. Although he said very little about him, he did tell me once how he felt when Kennedy announced that Americans were headed to the moon. He said that every boy in his school thought about being an astronaut and, for a while, it's all they talked about. Kennedy used his platform as president to inspire a nation to rally around a cause, and, even though the Soviets beat the United States in several phases of the race to the moon, Neil Armstrong and Buzz Aldrin planted our flag on the surface of the moon, and Americans declared victory in the space race.

When I was growing up, it was Ronald Reagan. I was ten years old when Reagan was shot, and our teachers turned on every television in the school. Everything stopped as a room full of elementary school students stared at the screen, watching Reagan walk into the hospital, and then trying our best to follow along as the news anchors gave us updates. I remember his meetings with Gorbachev, his Star Wars initiative, and, if I live to be one hundred years old, I will never forget his appearance in front of the Berlin Wall, challenging Gorbachev to "tear down this wall." Although he wasn't the president when it happened, I sat in my living room as an eighteen-year-old, watching MTV's coverage of Germans doing just that, tearing down the Berlin Wall. In almost every way, Ronald Reagan made me believe that I could do anything I put my mind to, and he will always be my second favorite president, right behind George Washington.

As I was preparing to write this chapter, I spent two days considering the question: Who is inspiring my kids? I wasn't concerned with whether or not they were being inspired to greatness, but, simply, from whom did they get their inspiration? The list was short. Rebecca, the oldest, said she is inspired by her own ambition, but there are some strong women, like Reese Witherspoon (her example) that inspire her. Riley, the second oldest and Rhett, the youngest, both said they couldn't think of anyone, and they try to inspire themselves. Hannah, our third oldest said it was her parents that inspire her (And that, folks, is how you get priority inclusion in Dad's last will and testament). Finally, our second youngest, Reese, said that Dwayne "The Rock" Johnson inspired him because of his work ethic. Not a bad list, but not a great list either. Not because Jessica, me, or The Rock aren't worthy to inspire others. It's not who they said…it's who they didn't say. There weren't any poets, inventors, astronauts, teachers, or presidents on their list. I'm not saying this is right or wrong, but it's a little concerning that, outside of our home, my kids either aren't inspired or they are inspired by celebrities. I'm not sure what kind of future we have if celebrities are the people that inspire us.

Not fully satisfied with the kids' answers, I took to Twitter and tweeted the following: "Who, specifically, has inspired you to either do better or be better?" After posting the tweet, I got my credit card out and paid $50 for the tweet to be "promoted." I am very pleased to report to you that the total number of responses to this paid tweet was (drum roll please) zero. It would have brought me more pleasure if I would have set $50 on fire and danced around it. My dad didn't raise a quitter, so I texted the same question to twenty-three people I am on a first-name basis with, and forty-eight hours later, only Kareem said his parents were and continue to be his inspiration. His was the only response, so I followed up with many of the twenty-three people I texted, and their answers were, essentially, "I couldn't think of anyone." Although the survey of my kids, my failed appeal to Twitter, and the survey of my friends are grossly unscientific, I discovered that those closest to me had no dominant inspiration in their lives. I think that's a problem.

Finding Washington

What has happened to us? Even though we aren't perfect, the United States is still a beacon of hope to people all around the globe. Although we have people in our country that have romanticized socialism and totalitarianism, the simple truth is that no one is trying to break into those countries. Cuba, located ninety miles from

Florida, is a communist country. No one that lives in Florida is trying to turn a 1952 Chevrolet Bel Air into a boat to make it to Cuba. Yet, Cubans will try almost anything, regardless of how dangerous it is, to get to America. We still have what it takes to inspire, but I'm afraid that our window is closing. But it doesn't have to.

In order to *find Washington* and become an inspiration to the next generation, we must make some changes. First, and this is important, *put your phone down! Turn Netflix off! Get off Facebook!* For the love of all that is holy, *get off Facebook!* Our addiction to technology is real. It's not funny anymore, and I am no exception. One of the negative consequences of our addiction is that we aren't engaging in activities that inspire. Like robots, we go to work, come home, and veg out until we fall asleep with our phone in our hand, and then get up and do it again the next day. You and I aren't going to inspire anyone watching TikTok videos.

Secondly, it's time to rediscover the meaning of sacrifice. I know we all sacrifice for our kids, but I'm talking about a different level of sacrifice. I'm talking about using your Saturdays for more than mowing the lawn. There are probably hundreds of charities in your community that would do backflips if they got a phone call asking when and where you can volunteer. We can genuinely inspire the next generation if we begin spending our time for the good of others.

Oh, and take the kids with you when you volunteer. Look, I know your precious babies are going to complain. That's what kids do. They complain about how unfair life is, and, frankly, I would be disappointed and surprised if they didn't. However, something will happen to your kids over time. They will learn that there is joy in serving, and they will be inspired by you and the people they meet along the way to be better and do better. I don't have a complicated algorithm, folks. This isn't rocket surgery. The next generation will receive their inspiration from pop singers, actors, or influencers (whatever the heck that is) if we don't become the inspiration they are looking for. I'm providing the following list of charities as a way to get you stimulated to think about serving.

- Habitat for Humanity: habitat.org

- Boys and Girls Club of America: bgca.org
- Compassion International: compassion.com
- Feeding America: feedingamerica.org

Volunteering for charity work isn't the only way to inspire others. Have you ever considered running for a local political office or serving on a government-sponsored board? You should. Most every city and county government have a list of boards and authorities you can serve on as a way to get involved in your community, and God knows we need regular people serving in elected office. The point here is not to list every way we can be an inspiration to others, but to stimulate our thinking. Washington found a way to motivate his troops when most of them had probably checked out and were ready to go home. It's not too late for us to sacrifice some of our time and use the gifts and talents God gave us to inspire the next generation. We know they're watching us, so let's give them something inspirational to remember us by.

CHAPTER 7

Character

4.5 Out of 10

I'm going to be honest with you. On a scale from one to ten, with ten representing extremely handsome and one representing butt ugly, I'm a solid four. Give my wife a glass of wine, and I'm a 4.5 for about a half hour. My wife, on the other hand, is a solid ten. Probably an eleven. Most husbands I know think of their wives this way, and they should, but mine *really* is a ten. She'll object, but that's because she's also humble. Aside from her external beauty, there are several things that attracted me to Jessica. First, she takes her faith seriously, which is important to me. Secondly, and this is important, she is attracted to fours. Third, she is extremely loyal. If she loves you, she really loves you. This is evident in her love for me and the kids, her dad, our pets, and, God, please forgive her, the Florida Gators. Lastly, she's a ten. Probably an eleven.

If you ask my kids to describe me, they will say a variety of things. I have a good sense of humor, and I love to joke around. My kids do not have to go to the internet for memes; I supply them as a free service. My sons are learning how men joke with one another outside of the presence of Mom, and the girls and I have can be found having a philosophical conversation about almost anything. Reese is the sports nut and a Gator fan like his mom, so he and I talk sports...a lot. The kids know that my favorite job is teaching, even though it pays next to nothing, and they know that I enjoy my alone time. They would also tell you that I have a quick temper. When something is bothering me, I get quiet, and it is rumored that I have used profanity when I get angry, but this report is unconfirmed. They will tell you that I would rather be in the woods hunting hogs or deer or preparing to hunt hogs or deer than anything else in the world. That would be the forest for all of you non-Southerners. And they would tell you that I love their mother more than oxygen.

If you ask them to describe Mom, you get a different picture altogether. Jessica is steady as a rock. She loves a good book or a football game, *cannot* sit still and, therefore, is always cooking or cleaning. True story: After spending all day in the clinic seeing patients, my bride will walk in the door, put her purse and computer down, and then start sweeping or cleaning something. If me or the kids walk to the mailbox and back, we think we deserve an extended break. Not Jessica. She is always on the move. Her one guilty pleasure is a good nap, and, trust me, she can nap like it's her job! She enjoys simple pleasures and wants to travel the world. The thing that makes Jessica feel most fulfilled is serving others, particularly the less fortunate or on the mission field, and her entire paycheck would go toward helping others if it wasn't required to fund the needs of our large family. She is *the* essential member of our family, and our kids will ignore me all day. But as soon as Jessica walks in the door, they are suddenly in desperate need of a parent. The kids and I don't have to look beyond her for an example of integrity, but, coupled with that, she has character, which is what I want to talk about in this chapter.

Fox Chase

A few days after Washington's surprise attack and victory at Trenton, Lord Cornwallis left a smaller force to guard Princeton and marched his Redcoats toward the Continental Army. As Cornwallis positioned his troops around Trenton, he knew that Washington was trapped by the Delaware River on one side and King George's finest soldiers on the other. Although several of Cornwallis' officers advised him to attack immediately, he thought it best to rest the troops from their weary march. Washington was, after all, trapped.

Meanwhile, Washington, aware of his precarious situation, was busy plotting his next move. While it was tempting to use the victory to rally his troops, Washington knew that the men were exhausted, hungry, and lacking supplies, so he decided the best option was to try and escape. However, he also knew that if Cornwallis' troops were camped outside of Trenton, it meant that two potential British targets were left vulnerable. The first was the town of Princeton. If Washington could slip by Cornwallis undetected, he could take Princeton almost as easily as he took Trenton. Beyond that, however, was the town of New Brunswick, which was where the British kept their supplies and £70,000 of British coin that, if captured, could solve many of Washington's problems. Washington knew what he had to do.

Washington commanded four hundred of his troops to remain in Trenton while the remainder of the army escaped. The men left in Trenton were instructed to busy themselves tending campfires and loudly digging trenches to ensure the British that the Americans were preparing for a fight. Meanwhile, sometime after midnight, Washington's men wrapped their oars and wagon wheels in rags to muffle the sound and crossed the Delaware River, escaping sure defeat while the British slept peacefully in their tents.

Around dawn the next day, the freezing and exhausted American troops formed into their lines and began the march towards Princeton. The biggest obstacle that lay in front of Washington in his campaign against Princeton was the Stony Brook Bridge, located about two miles outside of town. General Hugh Mercer was dispatched with a small detachment of men to take the bridge. Mercer guided his men through the forest, and, just as he arrived at the bridge, he spotted the British troops led by Colonel Charles Mawhood and began engaging them with musket fire. Mawhood immediately instructed his men to charge with bayonets, and, as Mercer was organizing his men for a response, he was overtaken by seven British soldiers, and killed immediately.

When Mercer fell, his troops immediately began to retreat toward Washington's position. When Washington saw his troops retreating, he shouted for them to attack and, to their amazement and shock, put his horse in a full gallop toward the advancing British. No one could believe what they were seeing. Washington was out in front of his soldiers, waving his hat and shouting for them to follow. To the British soldiers' surprise, there was the leader of the Continental Army, alone and unprotected, galloping his horse toward them.

While I could not determine the exact number of British troops fighting in this battle, we do know that Mawhood was commanding 1,400 British troops that day, so it is reasonable to assume that the force protecting the bridge would have been several hundred. And Washington was on his horse, riding full speed toward them. The British soldiers pointed their weapons at George Washington and fired. Smoke from ignited gun powder was so thick that neither side could see properly, but all watched in amazement as George Washington circled back towards his troops, without a scratch on him, shouting for them to attack. At the sight of the American attack, the British retreated across the bridge and headed for Princeton. When giving the order to make chase, Washington shouted for his men to pursue because "it's a fine fox chase, my boys!"[16] When the battle was over, five hundred British lay dead, and the Continental Army suffered fewer than fifty casualties.

Kiss My

Unless you're skipping ahead, you've already been through the chapter on integrity. I'll get to the differences between character and integrity in a minute, but first, let's revisit integrity. In chapter three, I said that "a person with integrity is a whole person...not divided or constantly conflicted, not knowing which choice to make. A person with integrity knows what is right and does what is right." That definition actually encompasses the definition of character as well because you can't have one without the other. If someone possesses little or questionable integrity, then that person usually displays equally low or questionable character. Since my definition of integrity encompasses the idea of wholeness or the absence of a divided moral com-

---

[16] https://paw.princeton.edu/article/battle-princeton

pass, both the quality of integrity and character must agree. To help us understand the subtle difference between integrity and character, we will define the latter as the outward display of a multiplicity of ingredients that make up integrity. Character, then, is the expression of someone's real values or vices. If integrity is who you are when no one is looking, character is who you are when they are looking.

I'm not splitting hairs here. Character is important because it helps us distinguish between authentic and counterfeit integrity. Imagine if, during World War II, a person was outspoken about the atrocities of the Holocaust. This person encouraged his neighbors to hide Jews and resist Nazi efforts to capture them or move them to the ghetto. To Jews and others, this person would seem to exhibit immense integrity. Imagine now that a Jewish neighbor approached this same man and asked for help hiding his family from the Nazis, but, in response, the man said it was too risky, and he didn't want to jeopardize his family's safety. We would surmise that this person's supposed integrity was counterfeit. He appeared to have integrity, but when given the chance to display it, he revealed through his actions…through his character…that he had little to no integrity at all. Character is how we determine the depths of someone's integrity.

In 2010, I was elected to the Lowndes County Georgia Board of County Commissioners. Although the voters had decided to expand the county commission, at the time I served, there were four of us: three commissioners elected by their districts and a county chairperson elected by all voters in the county. Our commission was divided evenly with two Republicans and two Democrats, and I was one of the Republicans. If you can remember the political landscape of our nation in 2010, Republicans in this country were a bit divided between average, everyday Republicans and Tea Party Republicans.

I was all in as a member of the Tea Party faction of the party. To me, it was a revival of historic principles of our Republic that were being forgotten by the people we had been elected to public service. In order for me to serve on the county commission, I had to overcome several obstacles. Since I was running for an open seat, five other people decided to run as Republicans as well, which meant it was almost certain there would be a runoff between the top three candidates unless one person received over fifty percent of the vote. The winner of the runoff would face a Democratic opponent in November. Since the primary election was in the summer, I announced my candidacy in the spring as soon as the incumbent announced he would not seek reelection.

Even though Jessica and I both had good jobs at the time, funding an election without asking for donations was not a reality for me, so I did what all politicians do, and I solicited donations from supporters. I received substantial help from a few donors that really believed in me. I can honestly say that, without their help, I probably would not have finished first in the primary and then go on to win the runoff, much less the general election. After spending four of the most fulfilling years of my life on the Lowndes County Board of Commissioners, I honored my campaign promise to only serve one term, and I announced my intention to do so in a letter to my supporters, fellow commissioners, and the local newspaper. Not long after making my decision to forego reelection, the long-term state senator from our district announced that he would not be running for reelection either. Jessica and I discussed the prospect of me running for the State Senate ad nauseam. I solicited advice from some close friends, and more people than I could possibly count called and emailed, expressing their hope that I would run.

The rest of this story requires a bit of explanation. Not only did the election of 2010 see the formation of the Tea Party, but it saw a significant shift in Georgia State politics. After the 2010 general election, there was a serious defection from the Democratic Party by several members of the Georgia General Assembly, including one our representatives, Ellis Black, to the Republican Party. Ellis, like a lot of Georgians, was a lifelong Democrat. He had served our county as a member of the school board before making the move to the general assembly. As far as most voters were concerned, including me, Ellis Black was a good man that genuinely tried to serve all his constituents faithfully, and I can tell you from personal experience that he was one of the most available and responsive elected officials I ever encountered, regardless of party affiliation. Some members of our Tea Party group, including one of my donors, didn't like him because they didn't see him as an authentic Republican. When he switched parties, they saw it as opportunism and said "once a Democrat, always a Democrat." They didn't, however, say the same about Ronald Reagan, who also switched from the Democratic to Republican Party, but I digress. Shortly after I made my announcement to run for the State Senate, Ellis Black did as well, along with a newly elected member of the county commission, who resigned his newly elected seat to pursue the Senate.

The race was on. The three of us began campaigning and, like a Vaudeville troupe, we took our song and dance routine on the road. Since there were three of us running, it was very likely that the primary election would eliminate one candidate, and the other two would battle it out in the runoff. I immediately began appealing to those that donated to my county commission campaign, and my biggest donors stepped up again and said they were with me. After a bevy of radio, television, and social media ads, I am very proud to say that when the results came in on election night, I came in third place. That would be last for those of you without a sense of humor. I lost big time, too. Like, imagine all the Rocky movies where he gets beaten to a pulp but then wins. It was like that except I didn't win. I did the opposite of winning. I lost like I was trying to lose.

The day after the election, I had two conversations. First, the former county commissioner, a fellow Republican, and Tea Party member called and asked for my endorsement for the runoff. Endorsements by losing candidates is important in runoffs because an endorsement is your way of telling your supporters who you hope they support. The other call was made by me to Ellis Black, telling him that he had my full support and endorsement, and I was at his service. That's right. Mr. Tea Party (me) chose to support someone that had been a Republican for a couple of years over a lifelong Republican. The "why" behind my decision would take too long to explain, and either person would have made a good Senator, but it had quite a bit to do with what I perceived to be the integrity and character of the candidates.

Not long after that and before the runoff, I was attending a meeting of the Lowndes County Republican Party. While at this meeting, I was approached by one of my donors, who urged me to endorse the other candidate. I laid out all the reasons why I simply couldn't do it, and then he said the words I will remember until the day I die: "If you don't do what I'm asking, I will make sure you never win another election in this state." I was floored. I mean, I had heard of this sort of thing happening but never imagined I would be on the receiving end of this kind of pressure. And here's why it came as such a shock. If you've ever attended a Tea Party meeting, then you know that one of the topics that dominates the discussion is how sick our political system has become and how our elected officials don't listen to the electorate—they only listen to lobbyists and interest groups that fund their campaigns.

I'm telling you; grassroots Conservatives and Liberals alike are nauseated at the extent to which our elected officials are bought. For goodness' sake, that's the main reason there's so much money in politics…so that those who donate money can steer the elected person in the direction that favors the donor. The electorate be damned! And after all the lectures from this donor to others about the problem with money in politics, here he was, doing the exact same thing to me. The shallowness of his integrity and the absence of his character was revealed. He was, in every way, a counterfeit. I'm not going to tell you how I responded, but it was a version of kiss my…After that meeting, I doubled down on my efforts to tell every human that would listen to me to elect Ellis Black, which is exactly what voters did in the runoff and, then again, in the general election.

Finding Washington

It isn't enough for us to say we have integrity. We must display our integrity through our character. I love this story about George Washington because it is one of the many examples where he displayed his integrity. It was one thing for him to wear his uniform to meetings of the Continental Congress and display his willingness to get into the fight. However, not one person in the room on the day he was asked to lead the army expected him to gallop toward the enemy like a madman to prove that he meant what he said. His display at Princeton was his integrity in action. Washington didn't just say he was all in on the cause…he proved it. At this point, I doubt any of us are surprised that Washington was the type of person that proved the depths of his integrity through his character, and most of us are familiar enough with his life that his integrity has never been a question, but his actions at Princeton certainly remove all doubt.

I know what you're thinking. You're thinking this might be a better story to highlight courage (or insanity), and you're not wrong. Like many of the stories about Washington, this story gives us insight into many of the virtues he possessed, and I think it's important that we understand two concepts. First, integrity isn't evident without character. It doesn't matter how much integrity you think someone has or how much integrity someone tells you they have until you see it displayed in their character. Character, then, is how we protect ourselves from trusting someone with counterfeit integrity. Secondly, someone doesn't have to be perfect to have good character. A mistake or a bad decision isn't the sum total of a person, but repeated actions over time do give us a picture of the level of someone's integrity. Character is something that is displayed over time.

There are several ways we can rediscover character in our culture and *find Washington* again. The first way is to stop putting our highlight reel on display via social media so that we create a persona that doesn't exist. During the recent demonstrations in response to George Floyd's death, camera crews were able to catch various wannabe social media influencers doing photo shoots to make their followers think they were demonstrating as well. These people were trying to convince their followers that they really cared, but their actions revealed they are narcissists and con men. We must stop this trend of pretending to be something we're not on social media. It's destructive.

Secondly, and this is important, start displaying character. No one is expecting you to ride toward gunfire like Washington did, but just like everything else you do that matters, it starts with small decisions. If you say you're going to mow the lawn, mow the lawn. If you say you're going to attend the event, attend the event. If you tell your kids not to use profanity, don't use profanity (I wrote that one for me). If you tell your family that lying is wrong, then stop telling white lies, which is just a made-up term to justify lying.

Next, and this involves all of us, don't let leaders get away with saying one thing and doing another. If a leader says that he or she has family values but commits adultery or treats their spouse like crap, they don't get to lead us anymore. Why? Because character is an indicator of integrity, and we deserve to be led by people of integrity. Likewise, make a commitment to yourself that you will consider both integrity and character when voting before considering political party (this isn't the first or last time I'll say this). In order for us to revive the importance of character, there has to be a radical transformation in our hearts and minds. The last thing we need are disingenuous acts of kindness meant to fool everyone into thinking we are a people of integrity. We need to *be* people of integrity so that the expressions of our integrity (i.e., our character) are authentic. Your kids, spouse, neighbor, coworker, the cashier at the grocery store, and the world is watching and, even if they don't know it, are starving for authenticity of character. The revival starts with us, and it starts today.

One last thing: do you remember my email? Here it is again for all the men because we know the women have better memories: richard@findingwashington.com. I want you to do me a favor and email me real world examples of authentic displays of integrity, and title your email *Examples of Character*. It could be examples of our kids, spouse, neighbor, or anyone else. Just don't email me examples of your personal displays of character. That would be bragging, and a person of integrity would never brag. I can't wait to hear from you.

CHAPTER 8

The Real Plague

Clayton Monroe Raines

I need to confess something. I think I'm ready to admit that I have something in common with former President Bill Clinton, and I'm not proud of it. It has nothing to do with interns. Get your mind out of the gutter. When he was president, I remember someone, either a talking head on television or in print, said that they believed he cared deeply about people groups but seemed to care little about individual people. I don't know if this is true or not, but even if it isn't, I identify with the characterization. Take homeless people for example. I care deeply about the plight of the homeless. I've researched the issue at great length, and if it weren't for religious people, especially Christians, the homeless in this country would have very few resources to help cope with being homeless.

Although Habitat for Humanity doesn't provide homes for homeless people, it does provide homes for those needing permanent housing, and it is one of the best solutions we have to provide affordable homes to Americans that might not be able to afford a home otherwise. However, as much as I care about the problem of homelessness, I do not have the same passion for individual homeless people. That doesn't mean I don't care; it just means I don't feel compelled to help every homeless person I see, and I can be guilty of not giving someone money and justifying it by telling myself it would just be used for drugs or alcohol. I'm getting better because

Jessica is the opposite, and she's helped me, but I struggle with having empathy at times.

I've also identified why I lack empathy. I am the grandson of Clayton Monroe Raines. There were very few of my formative years that weren't spent in close proximity to my grandfather, and because we had a family business, I was around him all the time. He's been dead for a few years now, and I miss him a lot. I think about him almost every day, and one of my most prized possessions is the folded flag from his funeral with a picture of him attached. In addition to spending time with him painting houses, I traveled extensively with my grandparents for many years in South Georgia and North Florida because my granddad was a musician in a bluegrass band. He would load up his bass fiddle (Google it), and we would attend bluegrass festivals, backyard parties, and jam sessions at campgrounds in the area.

Additionally, it seemed like all the band practices were at his house, and I would often attend these practice sessions just to be around the music. He must have been a very good bass player because he was always sought out by others, and he never lacked a band to play with. My present musical tastes are heavily influenced by him today. I remember in the late 1970s going to his house and listening to Conway Twitty, Loretta Lynn, George Jones, Johnny Cash, Willie Nelson, Waylon Jennings, Kris Kristofferson, and a host of other traditional and outlaw country music artists. When cable television made it to our town, I would stay up at night with him eating vanilla ice cream and watching Smokey and the Bandit or Hee Haw reruns. And on Sunday mornings, he would watch Oral Roberts, even though my grandfather was a Southern Baptist with no tolerance for Pentecostalism.

There was, however, another side to Clayton Raines. He could be the biggest jerk any of us has ever known. If there was a national association of jerks, he would have been their leader. He wasn't like that all the time, but when he decided to be that way, it was ridiculous. I remember once as a teenager that he and I went through a fast-food drive-through. When we got to the window and the sixteen-year-old girl with braces told him how much to pay, he used profanity at her and said he would pay when he got his food. I wanted to crawl to another universe.

He could also lack empathy and often, when hearing of someone's death, would remark negatively about that person's life and point out their faults. I remember late one evening when we were coming home from a bluegrass festival, we came upon a car overturned in a ditch. My grandad slowed down, and a bloody-faced teenager approached my grandad and asked for help. My grandfather, whom I loved and still love dearly, told that injured young man he couldn't do anything for him, and that he should try and use the phone at a house close by. He didn't offer to help, didn't inquire about the young man's injuries, and drove away while he stood in the road in obvious disbelief. I will never forget that night. Even though I would never lack empathy on that level, it doesn't come as any surprise to me that it's something I struggle with. Fortunately for us, George Washington did not struggle one bit with empathy.

Stocks and Stones

In October of 1777, the Americans were able to achieve perhaps their most significant victory of the war thus far by defeating the British at the Battle of Saratoga. This victory would prove to have enormous implications in two primary ways. First, because it yielded in the capture of over 5,000 British troops, the French finally began to seriously consider joining the Americans. Up to this point, the French weren't entirely certain the Americans had what it took to stand up to the British. Secondly, although it was a major victory for the Americans, it may have been the event which convinced the war's most infamous traitor, Benedict Arnold, to switch allegiances. Prior to Saratoga, Arnold was one of Washington's most able officers, but his commanding officer, General Horatio Gates, refused to credit Arnold for previous victories and even left his name entirely out of a report Gates issued to Congress. At Saratoga, Arnold was nothing short of a hero for his bravery and command of the troops. However, since he participated in the battle against his commanding officer's wishes, Gates purposely omitted Arnold's contributions and took all the credit for winning the battle himself when he submitted his report to Congress.

Unfortunately for Washington, the victory at Saratoga was short-lived. In November, he marched his army to Valley Forge, where they would spend the next several months being tested in ways that most free Americans today are unaware. When the troops arrived at Valley Forge, they were in the worst shape imaginable. Most of the soldiers did not have a tent, and because there were few blankets, many slept on the cold Pennsylvania ground with only rags to cover them. There were more soldiers without shoes than with shoes, and some of the troops' clothing was so tattered that they had to stay covered by rags or blankets to hide their nakedness. Food was also in short supply. The only real food the soldiers ate were fire cakes, which consisted of a little flour and water, baked in the ashes of a fire. Despite Washington's appeals to Congress, the states displayed little sympathy and simply said they were out of money. It is estimated that over twenty-five percent of the army died that winter by starvation, freezing to death, or succumbing to sickness related to the hundreds of diseased and rotting carcasses of horses that had starved but couldn't be buried in the frozen ground.

There were two major factors which led to the poor conditions of Washington's army. First, Thomas Mifflin, Washington's quartermaster (the officer responsible for procuring supplies for the troops), was embroiled in a controversy with some other officers to depose Washington and replace him with Gates or some other general. As a result of his preoccupation with deposing Washington, Mifflin significantly neglected his duties for most of 1777. In October, he submitted his resignation after the plot against Washington was halted, and although Congress accepted his resignation, they asked him to remain in his position until a replacement could be found. This meant that at a time when the Army was most desperate for food, shelter, and clothing, the Army had no one committed to the task with any sense of urgency.

It wasn't until Washington demanded that Congress replace Mifflin with General Nathaniel Greene that things began turning around for the Americans and supplies began arriving. Secondly, instead of accepting the near worthless Continental dollars, merchants chose, instead, to sell their supplies to the British, who paid with the British pound—a much more stable and valuable currency. Even with Mifflin in place, the plight of the American soldier would have been relieved much sooner had his countrymen not chosen to sell their goods to the British.

During that horrendous season in the life of the Continental Army, it seems that Washington was vexed on all sides. He was forced to watch his army freeze and starve while farmers in the surrounding area charged exorbitant fees for food. Additionally, he was forced to watch his men barter with each other for shoes and blankets that he thought should have been supplied in abundance by an ineffective, Congress-appointed quartermaster who was too busy trying to depose him to do his job. On December 3, he penned a letter to Henry Laurens and outlined the condition of his troops:

> "Full as I was in my representation of matters in the Commissary's department yesterday, fresh and more powerful reasons oblige me to add, that I am now convinced beyond a doubt, that unless some great and capital change suddenly takes place in that line this Army must inevitably be reduced to one or other of these three things. Starve—dissolve—or disperse, in order to obtain subsistence in the best manner they can. rest assured, Sir, this is not an exaggerated picture, and that I have abundant reason to support what I say.
>
> Yesterday afternoon receiving information that the Enemy, in force, had left the City, and were advancing towards Derby, with apparent design to forage and draw subsistence from that part of the Country,[1] I ordered the Troops to be in readiness, that I might give every Opposition in my power; when behold! to my great mortification, I was not only informed, but convinced,

that the Men were unable to stir on account of provision, and that a dangerous mutiny, begun the night before and which with difficulty was suppressed by the spirited exertions of some Officers, was still much to be apprehended for want of this Article.

This brought forth the only Commissary in the purchasing line in this Camp, and with him this melancholy and alarming truth, That he had not a single hoof of any kind to slaughter, and not more than 25 Barrells of Flour! From hence form an opinion of our situation, when I add, that he could not tell when to expect any.

All I could do under these circumstances was, to send out a few light parties to watch and harass the Enemy, whilst other parties were instantly detached different ways to collect, if possible, as much provision as would satisfy the present pressing wants of the Soldiery—But will this answer? No Sir: three or four days bad weather would prove our destruction."[17]

Washington went on to say:

"Notwithstanding which, and that since the 4th Instant our numbers fit for duty from the hardships and exposures they have undergone, particularly on account of Blankets (numbers having been obliged and still are, to set up all night by fires, instead of taking comfortable rest in a natural and common way) have decreased near 2000 Men, we find Gentlemen without knowing whether the Army was really going into Winter Quarters or not (for I am sure no Resolution of

---

[17] https://founders.archives.gov/documents/Washington/03-12-02-0628

mine would warrant the Remonstrance) repro-
bating the measure as much, as if they thought
the Soldiery were made of Stocks or Stones, and
equally insensible of Frost and Snow."[18]

In desperation, Washington penned a letter to every state but
Georgia, alerting them to his army's condition and asking them to
send supplies immediately. In the midst of this, the conspiracy against
him reached the ears of Congress, who decided to send a delegation
to investigate the claims that he was preparing to march his troops to
York, Pennsylvania, where Congress was meeting, and set himself up
as an American dictator. As distracting as the conspiracy was against
him, Washington decided that, rather than defend himself to the
visiting delegation, he would, instead, use it as an opportunity to
highlight the condition of his troops, even if it resulted in his removal
as commander in chief.

Washington called on Alexander Hamilton to assist him in
executing this risky move, and together, they penned a letter to the
delegation, which, when complete, was thirty-two pages long and
explained in great detail both the condition his army was in and
the devastating effects their condition would have for the Revolution
during the upcoming spring campaign if not addressed. When the
members of Congress arrived and received his letter and witnessed
the conditions of his soldiers, they were appalled. Additionally, while
investigating the claims against Washington, the committee became
trapped in the camp by a powerful snowstorm, which gave them an
opportunity to live exactly as the soldiers did, which none of the
committee members were prepared for.

At the end of the committee's visit, they were so overwhelmed
by, not only the conditions of the troops, but Washington's decision
to selflessly advocate for them instead of offering a defense against the
charges they came to investigate that they, not only made a recommit-
ment to him as their choice for commander in chief, but requested
that Congress approve all of the requests that he and Hamilton had

---

[18] Ibid.

outlined in their thirty-two page letter. It shouldn't come as a surprise to any of us that Washington had so much empathy for his troops that he risked losing his position to improve their condition. It was a selfless act which emanated from a heart filled with empathy for a group of men he had so much affection for.

Finding Washington

Now that I've mentioned empathy a few times, perhaps it would be a good idea to properly define it before going any farther. *Empathy* is defined as the ability to strongly identify with a person or people in a way that puts you in that person's shoes. It's more than compassion, which is feeling sorry for someone. When we're empathetic, we've imagined ourselves in a particular situation and can actually feel their pain. Generally speaking, I think the ability to empathize with others is disappearing among us. Am I alone here? I don't think so, and I can't sit idly by while we continue on this path toward callousness for others.

I don't mind telling you that my biggest obstacle to writing this section is trying to figure out how we got here. I am a firm believer that in order to fix a problem, you have to have a proper diagnosis. I guess spending sixteen years talking to doctors and nurses has taught me that. I must confess, however, that I have failed you. I tried blaming it on video games and movies, but that was just intellectual laziness. I don't think video games and violent movies are making us less empathetic. I just couldn't think of anything else, and I knew if I wrote that, parents would quote me when taking away their kid's video games. Lucky for you, I am married an eleven that's into fours. While enjoying a rare date night tonight without kids, Jessica gave me her opinion, and it lit up all of my sensors, letting me know she hit the bullseye. I'll try and sum it up for you.

We are a "scroll culture" (her words). Aside from our jobs, we don't really interact with people in person anymore. Even at church or social events, we barely interact in an authentic way. We scroll through pictures and profiles or watch thirty-second videos of people, then we're off to the next picture, profile, or video. People aren't people anymore…they're digital images displaying everyone's fantasy life. All we see is the beautiful picture of a happy family standing on the beach, but what we don't see is that five seconds before the picture was taken, the kids were fighting, and dad was yelling at the dog. It's all fake. All of it.

If I pulled up your social media profile, I would see your highlight reel, not the outtakes and bloopers. And we spend hours interacting with digital fantasies and almost no time engaging real people. No wonder we don't have empathy. We don't relate to real people anymore. How in the world could we have any empathy in this scroll culture? The reason Washington could empathize with his troops is because he lived with them. He interacted with them every day, and he could see their struggle. And as long as a starving, nearly naked, and barefoot army was only something described in a letter, Congress didn't get it either. It took George Washington and a snowstorm to elicit empathy from them, which is why I know it isn't video games and movies that are to blame for our disappearing empathy.

Now that we have a diagnosis, what is the treatment? While I'm not certain I have all the answers, I am convinced that we have to shut down the majority of social media engagement in our lives. Not only is social media draining our empathy, but it's also making us more negative. And I don't want you to think I'm pointing fingers here because I am just as guilty as you. I genuinely enjoy Twitter (the only social media platform I regularly engage), but I find myself sucked into its negativity and divisiveness after just a few minutes. I become angrier and less concerned with how my tweets might be used to tear someone down. Forget Covid-19; the real plague that's killing us is social media!

Guys…we have to shut it down and start intentionally engaging others again. Go meet your neighbors. I'm not talking about small talk while you're both getting out of your car either. I mean invite them over and share a meal. Don't just hug someone's neck at church and pretend like you and your husband weren't on the verge of a divorce on the drive over…be real with people. Stop being fake. Purposefully engaging others is how we get our empathy back.

It's how we begin seeing people as people again and stop being so judgmental.

It's time to email me again. I know I keep asking for it, but I'm not going to let you read this book, tell others how good or bad it is, and then forget about it. I want to *find Washington* again and all his virtues. If you haven't figured it out yet, *you* are the Washington I am trying to find, and so am I. I don't want you to read another chapter of this book until you reach out to someone you don't know that well or someone you've lost touch with and make real-world contact with them. Hopefully, restaurants and coffee houses will exist in our post-apocalyptic, post-coronavirus world, and I want you to use those to get to know people again. If someone lives too far, invite them to a Zoom meeting and have a virtual happy hour. Once you've done this, send me pictures with a note about the interaction. Be purposeful and take your kids. Make them interact too. We need this, and I need proof that you are taking this seriously. I can't wait to see your pictures. Email me at richard@findingwashington.com.

CHAPTER 9

Intermission

Dances with Wolves

I figure if you have stayed with me this long, then you have one of the following interests: 1) You love George Washington, and you are only enduring my writing style to get to the historical stories; 2) The moral decay of our society has you concerned, and you are desperately seeking an improvement; 3) You are fascinated by bad writing, and you keep reading to see just how bad it can get. Whatever the reason, thank you for hanging in there with me. To those of you in group 1, this chapter is for you.

When I was a teenager, I knew someone that went to a different school and, like many teens, she had a group of friends that she hung out with. There were two people in the group that didn't really go on a lot of dates, so the group decided to set these two up to go on their own date. When the highly anticipated night of the date came, the two decided they would play it safe and stick with dinner and a movie. While I don't remember which restaurant they went to, I will never forget which movie they saw. The couple decided they would see the season's biggest hit, which, in 1990, was *Dances with Wolves* starring Kevin Costner. If you haven't seen it, you should because it's a great movie about a United States Army officer who is assigned to a far western outpost and then, because he is all alone, develops a relationship with a wolf and a tribe of Lakota Indians, who eventually accept him as one of their own.

Although the movie is over three hours long, it's worth renting on Amazon. After the date, the happy couple was talking to their curious friend group about their evening, and, when asked about the movie, they said that it was pretty good but had a horrible ending. Since everyone in the group had seen the movie and loved it, they couldn't imagine what the two were talking about, so they asked them to explain. Their biggest complaint was that it just ended with no clarification regarding what happened to Kevin Costner's character, the Indians, or the wolf. Then it dawned on someone that these two lovebirds had never been to a movie with an intermission, so when the screen went dark and the word "Intermission" popped up on the screen, they thought it was over and left. That's right. They left during the intermission. I'm sure that story comes up at every class reunion and, you know what...it should.

I thought it would be a nice change of pace to make this chapter the intermission. In this chapter, we are going to take a break from discussing Washington's virtues and, instead, focus on one of the most outstanding characteristics he displayed at every turn: his incredible leadership ability. Since leadership isn't really a virtue, it technically doesn't fit, but since this is my book and I get to decide what's in it, we're going to talk about Washington's near superhuman ability to lead others.

A Word about Leadership

This isn't a book on leadership, but since George Washington was the ultimate leader, we have to talk about it. Before we do, however, I need to get a few things out of the way regarding leadership. If you regularly consume books and podcasts on leadership, then you have already identified about a dozen examples of Washington exhibiting leadership traits. If you aren't into that sort of thing, then you probably need a quick primer and maybe the name of a good resource to get you started. Although there are more than a handful of good resources, I think John Maxwell's *Developing the Leader*

Within You[19] is the first place anyone interested in understanding leadership or developing themselves into a leader should go. I would even encourage you to skip any other leadership book you might be interested in and read Maxwell first.

The reason I recommend Maxwell as the first stop on the journey to understanding leadership is because his definition is the best I've seen. I don't want to give too much away in case you've stopped reading my book and are searching Amazon to find Maxwell's, but he defines leadership as influence, which is the most comprehensive definition I've found. Jesus and Hitler were both leaders because of the influence they had on others, but there are a multitude of other qualities that determined what kind of leader they were. The following stories from George Washington's life will, not only highlight his remarkable leadership, but also various other attributes associated with leadership that make him one of history's most remarkable leaders.

There's one more thing that I need to point out. Up to now we have focused on Washington as a soldier and General. In the chapters that follow, we will highlight some of the virtues he displayed after the Revolutionary War, starting with this chapter. This was a tough call for me because there's so many more stories from the war that I would like to discuss. In fact, I almost titled this book *Finding General Washington* but, in the end, decided that we needed to look at his entire career for guidance and inspiration. He was a complex man, and although he remained committed to fighting for his country as a soldier, it only represents a fraction of who George Washington really was.

October 19, 1781

Almost seven years after the first shots were fired at Lexington and Concord, at 2:00 p.m. in the afternoon on October 19, 1781,

---

[19] Since *Developing the Leader Within You* was written in the early 1980s, Maxwell has updated it. The updated version is *Developing the Leader Within You 2.0*. Although I haven't read *2.0*, you should start with that edition since it's updated with more relevant information.

Lord Cornwallis surrendered his 8,000 British and Hessian troops as prisoners of war to General George Washington. Actually, that's not what happened. Rather than meet Washington and surrender his own sword, Cornwallis sent word that he was unavailable, and, instead, sent Brigadier General Charles O'Hara to attend the surrender ceremony. Washington gave the honor of accepting the British surrender to General Benjamin Lincoln. As the surrendering soldiers laid down their arms and marched past the Americans, their fife and drum corps solemnly played "The World Turned Upside Down."

When news of the surrender reached England, King George III was so distraught that he had formal papers drawn up for his self-removal as the sovereign King of England. At the same time, the prime minister resigned his post in disgrace. The American defeat of the mighty British army was, perhaps, the most unlikely and shocking turn of events anyone in western civilization could have imagined. Admittedly, victory came as a direct result of French assistance, but it's important to remember that France resisted intervention until they thought the Americans might win the war. And although the American colonies had managed to assemble some of the brightest minds in the world to lead their new country, the world only recognized one name: George Washington.

If we're using Maxwell's definition that leadership is influence, then I think the point has been made that Washington was more than just a leader. Rather, he is *the* ultimate example of leadership. Strike that. He is *the* example of phenomenal leadership! It's what Washington did with his influence that sets him apart from the greatest patriots of the cause. He wasn't as intelligent as Thomas Jefferson (and certainly not as immoral) or as well read as John Adams. He didn't share Benjamin Franklin's wit or brilliance, and he wasn't half the communicator that Thomas Paine was, but he managed to lead a starving and barefoot army with almost no supplies or munitions against (literally) the most powerful army and navy on the planet.

He lost more battles than he won, and until later in the war, his most significant contribution to the war effort was running from the enemy. His authority was constantly undermined by subordinates, and at least two of his officers committed outright treason. I would argue that, prior to his first military engagement against the British, the average military strategist would have put his odds somewhere around zero percent chance of winning. Yet, with the advantage of hindsight, we can read history with a sense of anticipation and even excitement that, regardless of how bad things looked for Washington and his ragtag army, it all works out in the end. Since this book is not about his leadership qualities, I don't want to overwhelm you with dozens of examples, but from my perspective, there is one primary characteristic which Washington regularly displayed that assisted him in becoming the leader we all know him to be: Courage.

Liberty to Step Back

When I tell you that Washington had courage, what I really mean is that he exhibited what appears to me to be an aversion to fear. He was fearless, but not in a way that we are familiar with. When we see examples of fearlessness, it's usually in the form of a daredevil that performs death-defying stunts, or when Steve Irwin would reach down and grab a venomous snake by the tail. While Washington's brand of courage shared certain elements of these examples, his was, in another way, entirely different. Washington didn't exhibit courage for courage's sake or to impress. Rather, his acts of courage were born from having laser focus on his goal.

We have already highlighted instances where he fought from his horse during the French and Indian War and again at the Battle of Princeton, but these are but two examples of instances where George Washington displayed remarkable courage and disregard for his own personal safety and well-being. It was such a common occurrence that his officers constantly protested against his courage. After the Battle of Princeton, Benjamin Harrison wrote to his friend Robert Morris that "every officer complains of his exposing himself too much."[20]

---

[20] https://books.google.com/books?id=q46RzzzlmWgC&pg=PT60&lpg=PT60 &dq=benjamin+harrison+%22every+officer+complains+of+his+exposing+ himself+too+much%22&source=bl&ots=ZS9CZ4yZKF&sig=ACfU3U3o PLEK01ay4q3ZDCxecwnb2JCAlg&hl=en&sa=X&ved=2ahUKEwiUodDSsd _qAhXCoXIEHY06DhEQ6AEwAHoECAQQAQ#v=onepage&q=benjamin

Quite literally, the biggest complaint that the average officer had of the commander in chief was that he seemed to have no regard for his own safety and would exhibit courage in a manner that frightened them.

There is another story from John Ferguson, a major in the British Army and a very accomplished rifleman. Prior to the Battle of Brandywine, Ferguson was moving in the trees close to the Continental Army, looking for troop placements or easy targets. During this mission, Ferguson reports that he saw two Americans on horseback and, rather than shoot two defenseless men, decided to call out to them, hoping to trigger a response which would justify telling his men to fire. Ferguson did not find out that one of the men was George Washington until sometime later, but he testified that when Washington saw him with his musket raised, he simply stared blankly at him for a moment and then slowly turned around and walked his horse in the opposite direction, with no sense of urgency or panic. Ferguson said, "I could have lodged half a dozen of balls in or about him, but it was not pleasant to fire at the back of an unoffending individual, who was acquitting himself very coolly of his duty, so I let him alone."[21]

On another occasion, during the siege of Yorktown, Washington was standing near Reverend Israel Evans, one of the Continental Army chaplains, looking through field glasses at the entrenched British army, located less than two hundred yards away. The British were firing cannons at Washington's position, and the cannon balls were exploding so closely to his and the reverend's position that it was spraying dirt on them. Evans marveled that the general didn't flinch or look in the direction of the exploding munitions. In fact, he reported that Washington didn't even lower his field glasses but continued observing the enemy as if nothing happened. During this same siege, he was standing with Colonel David Cobb in an area which the British had zeroed in on with musket fire and mortars.

%20harrison%20%22every%20officer%20complains%20of%20his%20
exposing%20himself%20too%20much%22&f=false
[21] Ibid.

As the musket balls whizzed by Cobb, much like Reverend Evans, he suggested that the general retreat to a safer position to which Washington quipped, "Colonel Cobb, if you are afraid, you have liberty to step back."[22]

Finding Washington

I hope you don't think that I'm suggesting that a leader isn't a leader unless she is willing to stare down the wrong end of a rifle barrel and simply stroll away. That's not the point of sharing these stories, and the last thing I want is for someone to read this and think that in order to properly lead, one must exhibit an absence of fear in the face of certain death. The type of courage Washington exhibited is rare. My friend Eric and I were talking about this today, and as a veteran of the war in Afghanistan, he said that he's met a few of these fearless types, and they're pretty scary. In other words, this specific type of courage is rare, but that doesn't mean courage should be rare. I think to fully understand the kind of courage we need to revive in our culture, it would benefit us to understand where Washington's unusual and celebrated courage came from.

I think a lack of fear has always been a part of Washington's personal ethos, but I believe the way he displayed his courage in moments like the ones I've highlighted in this chapter can be traced back to the Battle of Monongahela during the French and Indian War. If you remember from previous chapters, this was the battle that resulted in Washington having multiple horses shot out from under him and at least three bullet holes in his coat. This is the battle that caused local Native American religious leaders to issue a prophecy about him and his future as the leader of a great nation. Although I

---

[22] https://books.google.com/books?id=fWH01rQHuR4C&pg=PA253
&lpg=PA253&dq=%22if+you+are+afraid,+you+have+liberty+to+step
+back%22&source=bl&ots=Lq6Fl1qVqw&sig=ACfU3U3qCPZUiti
t0u5-UGYLADGKSaacUg&hl=en&sa=X&ved=2ahUKEwjnibLeud_
qAhUmlXIEHehKAsg4ChDoATAEegQICRAB#v=onepage&q=%22if%20
you%20are%20afraid%2C%20you%20have%20liberty%20to%20step%20
back%22&f=false

think Washington possessed a large measure of courage before this battle, I think in the aftermath, he began to sense that God had specific plans for him, which did not include dying on the battlefield.

I haven't said much about Washington's faith yet because I was saving it for this chapter. If you quiz ten historians about Washington's religious beliefs, you will likely get ten different answers. But if they are genuine historians and not revisionists, they will unanimously agree that Washington possessed genuine Christian faith, and he was not, like some Founding Fathers, a secularists or deist that simply thought God put the world in motion at creation and now simply observes things from afar. One of the great things about technology, at least for our purposes, is that you can visit the Library of Congress (loc.gov) and view most of Washington's existing letters written during his career. It won't take you very long to see that on several occasions, Washington appealed to Providence as either a reason for a certain victory or escape and a reason to hold out hope for the future.

Providence isn't a word we use very often so it might be helpful to define it. In many ways, Washington used the term as a synonym for "God." By referring to the divine as "Providence," he was referring to the belief that God was active in the affairs of men, and, in many cases, active in the direction of his personal life. He saw God as a wise creator and one which would judge men at some point in history. Washington was extremely private about his religion and could often be found kneeling with an open Bible and praying in solitude. He was very active in the Anglican Church prior to the war and after he became President. I believe that Washington's courage stemmed from his belief that God had spared him at Monongahela and was providentially guiding the American colonies toward independence and victory in the war against England.

If I'm right (and I think I am), Washington's courage was less about his lack of concern for his own safety and more about his belief that God had a purpose for him beyond the war. I want to be clear here…in American Evangelical circles, one could misinterpret what I just said and think that Washington was super spiritual and so in touch with God that he knew he couldn't be killed. That would be awesome if it were true, but that's unlikely. What is more likely is that

George Washington believed in God, believed God was involved in the activities of humans, and that the independence and self-governance of an American nation was part of God's ultimate plan, and God intended to use Washington in securing America's freedom. I think Washington sensed God's providential hand at Monongahela, and as the conflict with England became more and more certain, Washington began to understand his role in God's divine plan, so he put on his Virginia militia uniform and attended those early sessions of the Continental Congress, silently awaiting the bittersweet call he knew one day would come.

So what does that mean for us? I'm going to be brutally honest here. I think this means that the best leader is the one that has a sense of divine purpose. I'm not talking about a theocrat or someone that has experienced some prophetic or apocalyptic event that they think gives them a mandate to lead. I'm not talking about religious zealots or cult leaders. I'm talking about someone that has a sense that God created them for a purpose that is aligned with divine ethics and imperatives. This type of leader is easy to spot because he or she is selfless, humble, and others-oriented. The leader that is aligned with God's purposes won't be self-serving. Even if they have narcissistic tendencies (leaders often do), it will not be their most striking feature, and this type of leader won't be a sounding board for others.

Leaders that have a sense of divine purpose often walk to the beat of a different drum and are more interested in unifying than dividing. Leaders that lead the way George Washington did will influence others by the courage they display through leading by example. The courage to lead by example is often more difficult than one might think. It takes great courage to think independently and then act accordingly. People with courage attract enemies the same way Washington did, often from among those who masquerade as supporters. However, when a leader's courage comes from a divine calling to serve rather than to be served, it makes them nearly impervious to challenges or betrayals, and, not unlike Washington's instinct to charge forward thoughtless of his own safety, courageous leaders serve and speak truth with no fear of consequences.

Lead by example. That's what George Washington did. He displayed courage because he sensed that his life was less about him and more about those he served. He never asked his soldiers to do anything he didn't prove by example that he was willing to do. I don't know about you, but that's the kind of leadership I'm longing to see in our country, and that's the kind of leader I've always tried to be. That's the kind of leader I want you to be. I don't care if you are in a leadership position or not. I want you to lead courageously with a sense that God created you to be a part of his plan for this world. I want to tell you a quick story, and then we'll move on from our intermission.

I work three jobs. My first job, as you already know, is in sales, but there's more to it than that. I don't actually work for the company I tell everyone I work for. I am a contract sales representative, which means I work for a company that provides sales reps to other companies. This means that when I go to work every day, I am quite literally on the bottom rung of the ladder. There is no career path forward for me. None. I exist so that the parent company doesn't have to lay off their own people, which has resulted in me getting laid off three different times, and just this past week, they cut both our salaries and bonuses so that they would not have to do that to their people. Performance doesn't matter.

Last year, I was the number one sales rep in my division. As a contract sales representative, we are little more than chess pieces to move around on the board, with zero consideration for our livelihood or family. On my other two jobs, I am an adjunct instructor, which means I teach classes as needed for two different colleges, and I am not guaranteed a salary or even a class to teach each semester. I exist to save both the colleges money. Adjuncts aren't full-time, permanent employees, so they are expendable. It's important that you understand that I have zero authority on any of my three jobs and have no path forward for any type of career advancement. There is no title after my name that denotes authority, and I am not eligible for one no matter how well I perform.

This means that, if you're reading this, it's impossible for you to be on a lower rung of the ladder than me. Maybe you are on the bottom like me, and maybe you're a little higher up. As it relates to courage and leadership, none of these circumstances matter. I make it a point to lead where I can. I find ways to lead. I pray for wisdom and then exercise that wisdom when it's time. Although I am on the lowest rung, I have established myself as a leader. The company that has laid me off three times has also found a way to bring me back each time. Why? Because I have a sense that God has placed me in this role for a purpose.

I am an advocate for the patients who take our medicines, I am a resource for the doctors, nurse practitioners, and physician assistants who prescribe our medicines, and I make it my business to know as much as the most intelligent physician out there about the human body so I can teach it back to my coworkers, thereby making all of us better. I'm not the guy in charge, but I have chosen to lead where I can and when I can.

As an adjunct instructor, I lead in the classroom. I don't just show up for class, phone in a lecture I've given fifty times, and then hope students don't bother me. I partner with my students. One hundred percent of my students have my cell phone number, and we text regularly. God has put me in these students' lives for a purpose, and I will not allow them to fail. If a student receives a failing grade in my class, then they were trying to fail. I love my students, and they love me, even if they disagree with me. I tell them the truth but then tell them to learn to think for themselves, and they all tell me that other teachers don't care as much as I do. My low status as an adjunct has no bearing on my ability to lead in a way that others will not. Why? Because I have a sense that God has put these students in my life for a reason, and for at least one semester, I want those students to see what it's like to live with divine purpose and courage.

I want you to lead. I don't want you to make excuses about your lack of opportunity to lead. We have a leadership vacuum in our country, and I want that to change. I'm tired of being a nation of fools and sheep led by idiots with no courage. I'm tired of leaders changing their ethics based on the way the cultural winds may be blowing. I want you...yes, you...to sense God's providential hand in your life, and I want you to think about others more than you think about yourself, and I want you to lead with courage.

End of intermission.

You may begin the next chapter.

Chapter 10

Baby and Bathwater

Hard Truth

This is a tough chapter to write. I don't have any humorous stories from my childhood or comedic anecdotes to make this easy, so I'll get to the point. George Washington owned slaves. He was a Virginia plantation owner, and he used slaves to perform the work on his plantation. I need you to hear me on this point because the truth is often muddied in an attempt to protect Washington's reputation. He was a full-fledged, one hundred percent owner of slaves. Regardless of whether he inherited them as a result of his marriage to Martha or any other means, the slaves belonged to him, and in the same way he owned the Mount Vernon plantation, George Washington owned other humans. Anything you read that tries to water down the reality that he owned slaves is trying to rewrite history or portray Washington in a way that even he did not try to portray himself.

I'm not going to defend George Washington. I'm not going to try and soften the issue by pointing out how kindly he treated his slaves compared to other slave owners. My goal here is to help you understand how this issue can be dealt with in a thoughtful and historically accurate manner without downplaying or disrespecting the plight of the enslaved. This issue is both simple and complex. It is simple because, as I've pointed out, Washington owned slaves. Whatever else you could say about this issue doesn't change the hard truth that he owned slaves. It is complex because Washington's relationship with his slaves and his struggle with the issue is incredibly revealing. Our treatment of the issue in this chapter will attempt to honor both extremes.

History Lesson

Reading and understanding history requires a different set of skills than those utilized in reading today's newspaper. The reason it requires a different set of skills is because we must be very careful about projecting modern sensibilities onto historical eras. That doesn't mean that right and wrong are subjective, but it does mean that people in a particular historical era may not hold the same values about an issue as modern readers do. There are at least two examples of this that I think help make the point: The Bible and abortion.

The Bible is the most read book in the world and will probably retain that title for many more years. Although the Bible is not primarily historical (it is primarily theological), the individual books that comprise it were written in historical contexts, with many of the stories and characters from the Bible intersecting well-known historical events. When we read the Bible, it is imperative that, before we try and interpret the theological meaning, we seek to understand the historical context. This includes the social, political, and economic climate. This includes various customs that were employed during the historical period in which the books were written, and it includes understanding (to the best of our ability) any cultural norms or trends that may have existed.

An example of how this impacts our reading of the Bible can be found in the story of Abraham. Early in the story of Abraham, we see that on two occasions, he lied and said that his wife wasn't really his wife out of fear that he would be harmed. He allowed his wife to be taken on two occasions to save his own hide. By our standards, this is reprehensible, but in 2000 BCE, women were considered property. Since Abraham is the father of Judaism, Christianity, and Islam, do we cast Abraham aside because he treated his wife with such disdain? No. We understand that, even though this was wrong, Abraham lived in a different era that adhered to a different ethic. It is highly unlikely that Sarah, Abraham's wife, thought her husband's actions were ethical at all! Fortunately, as we read through the pages of the Bible, we see theological movement on how adherents to the faith treat women, culminating in the New Testament admonition that, in Christ, gender and other distinctions based on dominance and control are nullified (Galatians 3:28). If we use the Bible as our example, we see how important it is to understand historical context, and this applies to the reading of any historical text.

The second issue which might help us understand historical context is abortion. If you're getting ready to stop reading because I'm going to talk about abortion, please stick with me a little longer. There have been approximately sixty million abortions in the United States since the Supreme Court handed down its decision in Roe vs. Wade in 1973. It is a highly divisive issue in our country, much like slavery was a highly divisive issue in the United States for decades before President Lincoln issued the Emancipation Proclamation. There are people in this country that think women should be able to have an abortion if they want one, and anyone that interferes is a bass-ackwards moron, who is denying a woman's human rights. There are others, like me, that think sixty million babies have been murdered in the new Holocaust. Those are the two extremes, and most Americans are somewhere in the middle and think we should let women choose but find a way to reduce the number of abortions. This middle way was also the predominant view regarding slavery in the earliest days of our country's history.

What if two hundred years from now, medical science advances to the point that we realize that abortion, at any stage of pregnancy is, indeed, taking an innocent life. What if two hundred years from now, Americans look back on us and marvel at how barbaric the practice of abortion was? What if future Americans rush into the streets and tear down statues of presidents and public figures that supported abortion. What if the Screen Actors Guild posthumously removes proabortion members from their roles, and streaming services remove any movies that promoted abortion or had actors in them that were outspoken proponents of abortion, and, in Congress, the Democratic Party says they were pro-life all along?

It is up to future generations to decide how to enforce cancel culture, but if you support abortion, you probably think this is unfair. It's not that you are for abortion as much as you are for women's rights, right? I mean, you do think women should consider other options in the third trimester, and if you could make your case to a future society, you would say, "I didn't think a baby in the first trimester was really human." In other words, you would be appealing to your own historical context and asking future Americans to take it into consideration before demonizing you. That's how we have to approach a discussion of the North Atlantic slave trade…by understanding historical context.

Slavery

Here's how our country currently views slavery: it is the worst possible thing that has ever happened in the course of human history and only concerns White Southern Americans and slaves from the African continent. That's it. No one cares that slavery has been a part of the human economy since before humans started recording history. No one cares that Republicans had to wage war against the Democrats to force them to free their slaves, and no one cares that there may be more than forty million people enslaved worldwide today, seventy percent of which are women and children. And if any Southern White American owned slaves, anything else that person has ever done must be erased from history, and those White descendants are to be judged for the sins of their ancestors.

You know what, slavery is one of the worst possible things that could happen to another human being. It robs a person of their humanity, separates families, perpetuates rape and molestation, exposes humans to violence and humiliation, and violates the divine freedom all humans are entitled to by our Creator. It is among the worst possible things a society could allow to exist, but it isn't in a category by itself. The way that some view slavery in our country represents either a complete lack of historical awareness or blatant hypocrisy. Take the current love affair with socialism, for example. Call me crazy, but I seem to remember that it was National Socialists in Germany that were responsible for the Holocaust? What about the horrors done in the former USSR? For those of you that went to public school, that acronym stands for the Union of Soviet Socialist Republics, and Nazi was what National Socialists in Germany called themselves in the 1940s. It is estimated that over forty million people died under the maniacal rule of Joseph Stalin. Using our current rage over slavery as a guide, we should immediately recall every elected politician serving at any level of government that shows any affection for socialism. After all, how could these people have anything to offer if they support a political system responsible for so much terror?

What about China? Not only does the Communist government in China persecute the Christian church and abuse their own citizens. At the dawn of the Communist Party's rule of China, Chairman Mao is credited for the murder of tens of millions of his citizens for outright or suspected dissent. Where are the calls for a complete economic separation from the Chinese? If a car company uses parts manufactured in China, we should immediately shut down those car companies, right? If your favorite soda comes in a can made in China, then, if we're being consistent, it isn't good enough to stop drinking that soda. We must destroy that soda company. If you continue driving cars made with Chinese parts or drinking soda that comes in cans made in China, then you are personally responsible for the death of tens of millions of Chinese people, and you should be fired from your job, evicted from your house, and your kids should be kicked out of school. I mean, if we're being consistent...right?

What about the abuse of young girls and forced marriage that is a cultural and religious norm in many countries? It is estimated that over six hundred million women are currently in marriages that they were forced into as children. Where's the outrage? If we find out that a country or a religion allows grown men to force girls into marriage, shouldn't we immediately suspend trade and travel between the USA and those countries? What about religions that, not only allow but celebrate child marriage? Using our current response to things that outrage us, shouldn't we ban the practice of that religion in our country? Corporations should immediately terminate all employees that practice that religion until the practice of child marriage ends and the women who were forced into marriage receive reparations. Before you get upset, I know the rules. We are only allowed to do that to Christians. Everyone else is off limits. But hypothetically, we're just being consistent, right?

Look, I'm not trying to be hard to get along with. I'm just trying to be consistent. And when I say that no one is outraged by child marriage or sex slavery, I don't literally mean that no one is outraged. Thank God for people who are outraged and are working to end these evils. You know who isn't outraged? The woke mob. They are singularly enraged by whatever their leaders tell them to be enraged about on social media and nothing else matters. If their glorious leaders tell them that statues need to be torn down, then, as dutiful followers, they tear them down until they are told to be outraged by something else. The elite leaders of the mob say that slavery in America was the worst kind of evil and anyone associated with the practice can't be trusted regarding anything else they may have thought or said, including the founders of this country. It's manufactured outrage and an attempt to institute mob rule, and that's not how we do things in a civilized republic.

People will read this chapter and accuse me of making light of slavery in an attempt to protect Washington's reputation. It doesn't matter that I've literally said that's not what I'm doing. The fact that I'm doing something other than bowing to the woke mob will brand me a racist. That's okay. You can't fix stupid. However, now that we've established that the current response to slavery is either unbalanced, not properly considered within its historical context, or, at worst, manufactured outrage, let's finally deal with George Washington, the slave owner.

George Washington and Slavery

At the time George Washington lived, the economy in the thirteen colonies and after the Revolutionary War was largely agrarian. In Europe, land was relatively expensive to acquire, but skilled labor for other industries, such as textiles, was more abundant. It was the opposite in the colonies; land was easy to get, but there was virtually no skilled labor. It is estimated that over eighty percent of all colonists supported themselves financially through agricultural enterprises. This meant that the colonies were able to export their goods to Europe and the West Indies. Products such as lumber, fish, and tobacco were readily available in America and highly coveted in Europe. Even though all the colonies (and eventually states) were primarily agricultural, the warm climate and rich soil in the Southern states provided longer growing seasons and more bountiful harvests.

The challenge for Southern farmers who grew their agricultural enterprises into large plantations was the scarcity of labor to work the plantations. Since that was the primary source of income for most Southerners, each family needed all their children working on family farms, which reduced the available workers and reduced the crops that could be grown. Most Southerners turned to labor supplied by African slaves to keep up with the demands of running large agricultural operations. Although there was a significant cost related to caring for slaves, it was still cheaper than importing labor from abroad. Thus, in one generation, the Southern economy went from large farms operated by families to large plantations operated by slaves.

If you have ever seen one of Amazon's warehouses, it is almost overwhelming. Just a few hours from where I live, Amazon built a 1.1 million square foot facility that employs a few thousand people to support the enormous challenge of keeping up with our desire to purchase goods online. It takes an army of people to keep up with the demand of providing those goods in a reasonable amount of time. Imagine for a moment that our demand for Amazon's products stayed the same, but Amazon couldn't find anyone to work in their facilities. That is what large farming operations were dealing with in the seventeenth and eighteenth centuries. Although there were other options available for labor, none were as lucrative as the option of slavery, so that's what nearly all Southern agricultural operations did. It didn't take long for the economy to adjust to the presence of slave labor in such a way that made trying to run a plantation without it economically unviable.

George Washington was a fully participating member in this economy. However, we know from his letters and other sources that

Washington eventually became persuaded that slavery was immoral and, in 1786, wrote:

> "I never mean (unless some particular circum-stance should compel me to it) to possess another slave by purchase; it being among my first wishes to see some plan adopted by the legislature by which slavery in the Country may be abolished by slow, sure, and imperceptible degrees."[23]

His close friend, the Marquis de Lafayette, worked tirelessly to help Washington develop a plan for emancipating slaves. Lafayette's most novel idea, which Washington supported, was to purchase land overseas and send slaves to work the land as free sharecroppers. Lafayette went as far as to purchase a plantation in French Guiana for that purpose and hoped to inspire other plantation owners to follow the same course of action. Washington, inspired by Lafayette, tried to lease large portions of Mount Vernon to Scottish farmers and convince them to use his slaves, which he would set free, as hired labor. Unfortunately, Washington's plan was not enacted, and, as we now know, the Southern states would fight and lose a war in an effort to keep their slaves. It may also be worth noting that, after the Revolutionary War, Washington committed himself to never buying or selling another slave. When he fell behind on his taxes, he refused to sell slaves to generate the necessary revenue. Washington allowed his slaves' families to grow, and he bore the cost of caring for more slaves than were needed to operate his plantation. Upon his death, Washington freed his longtime aide and companion, Billy Lee, and dictated that all Mount Vernon slaves be set free upon Martha's death.

---

[23] https://www.mountvernon.org/george-washington/slavery/washingtons-changing-views-on-slavery/

So What

Let's be clear, Washington doesn't get any brownie points for being a compassionate slave owner. That's like giving credit to a rapist because he told the woman he loved her. At the end of the day, Washington was a slave owner, and although he wrestled with the issue, he never did the right thing. It's a stain on his character, and one which he knew would adversely affect his legacy. It is noteworthy that he changed his views over time, and it is admirable that he had abolitionist sensibilities, but in the end, Washington let his slaves down, and he let future generations of Americans down. Does this mean, however, that everything Washington did should be thrown out? Of course not. That's how children think. It may surprise you to learn that in 1776, Phillis Wheatley, a former slave, corresponded with General Washington and even dedicated a poem to him, asking for divine guidance and protection. That's right. A former slave penned a poem to honor the slave owner George Washington. Do you know what this means? It means that slavery was a complicated issue in 1776, and even former slaves did not define George Washington by this one issue, and neither should we.

If you look closely at your heroes, you will discover that they are all soiled in some way. I am aware of only one person in history that escapes that description, and he was crucified for his beliefs. None of the men and women we look up to from our history were perfect, and it is illogical to toss the baby out with the bathwater by discounting someone's positive accomplishments (or hiding their failures) in an effort to show solidarity with people or issues of our own day. It is possible for me to tell you that Washington was a model of virtue, but he was also a slave owner. Those two things aren't mutually exclusive, and George Washington should be judged by the corpus of his accomplishments rather than the one issue, which people seek to define him by today. George Washington owned slaves, but he also led America to her independence and guided her through her infancy. Let's remember him for all these things.

I want to end this chapter by saying that even though Washington ultimately failed to do the right thing, he still provides a lesson for us if we're willing to learn. Washington lived and worked in an environment where few questioned the morality of slavery. After all, every great society in history up to that point embraced slavery. When Washington finally became convinced that slavery was immoral, he began openly discussing the need for a plan to abolish it and began searching for solutions to abolish slavery at Mount Vernon. It's tough to admit when we're wrong, especially when we realize that something we've believed for years is a lie, but that's what Washington did.

He spoke out against the prevailing Southern philosophy regarding slavery. I think it's fair to say he didn't speak loudly enough, and his slaves would certainly agree with that, but it's commendable that he didn't remain completely silent. I think there are at least two lessons here. First, don't be too proud to admit it when you're wrong. It takes a lot of maturity and emotional intelligence to admit error. Secondly, don't delay when given the opportunity to do the right thing. Washington didn't act swiftly enough to abolish slavery, and Americans have been paying a price for that error since the first slave ship arrived in North America. While I certainly understand that Washington's generation viewed slavery differently, once he determined that it was evil, he should have sought out a more universal solution. There's no reason that lesson doesn't apply with us as well.

I understand that this is a complex and emotional issue. You may be reading this and are outraged that I would even consider that Washington was anything less than a monster for owning slaves. I understand your outrage, but you must remember that we don't judge someone by their failures. We judge them for how they respond to failures. In eighteenth century colonial America, there was no abolitionist movement to speak of. Washington's peers did not share his enlightened view. If fact, other than John Adams, I'm not aware of many other Founding Fathers that were abolitionists. This doesn't absolve Washington, but it certainly gives historical context about an issue we have no personal experience with or firsthand knowledge of.

CHAPTER 11

Hope

I often wonder if my dad would be proud of the dad I've become. He and I are different in a lot of ways. I have much less patience with my kids than he had with me, and unlike him, I haven't made a habit of asking my kids to hold a flashlight while I work on a car at night. He and I are also the same. We are both fluent in sarcasm, and I take great joy in not ever giving my kids a straight answer about anything, just like he did with me. As I get older, I often think about the different conversations he and I would have and the different pieces of advice he would give. Although my dad was never in the military or in law enforcement, he always advised me to never sit with my back to the door in a restaurant. This way, he mused, I would always be aware of my surroundings, including who is coming or going. He also had lots of advice when it came to a career, none of which I listened to, and all of which I wished I had listened to.

It also seems like my dad would go through phases where he would give the same advice regularly. For instance, when I would do something stupid, and he would inquire why I did the stupid thing. I would often reply, "I don't know," to which he would reply, "If you don't know, then why did you do it? If you're going to do something stupid you should at least have a reason." Another of his favorites when I was a young teenager struggling in math, he would often ask if I was ready for a quiz or test, to which I would answer, "I hope so." His reply was always the same, and if I close my eyes, I can see his face and hear his voice as he would say, "Hope isn't a strategy...now get in your room and study." When I survey all his wise sayings and advice, I think that one has stuck the most and I have been committed to the notion that hope isn't a strategy for most of my life. However, I have a story about George Washington that gives me at least one reason to modify this advice, and I think my dad would agree.

The Virginia Plan

I have a sad confession to make: I was a college student before I learned the truth about the formative years of our young nation. By the time I graduated from high school, my knowledge of the Revolutionary period of the United States consisted of the Boston Massacre, the Boston Tea Party, the Battle of Lexington and Concord, the Battle of Yorktown and Washington's inauguration. That's it. That's the sum of what I learned about our eight-year armed struggle for independence against the world's preeminent superpower. The part of the story that was most surprising to me is just how fragile our young republic was. It's no secret that running a country without a monarch was a foreign concept in Europe, and the world watched our progress with great interest, and more than a few old-world countries were openly rooting for our failure. The scary part is that we came dangerously close to failing, but since there are no questions about the period between the close of the Revolutionary War and Washington's inauguration on high school standardized tests, not much is said about it in the classroom.

Here's what happened. In 1777, at the beginning of the Revolutionary War, Congress adopted the Articles of Confederation as our chief governing document. The articles created a confederation of states that ensured the individual states would have more authority than a central government. The practical consequences of this type of government are the states had all the power and rendered any notion of a national government powerless. During the years immediately following the Revolutionary War, states were, essentially, functioning as independent countries and would even issue tariffs. The lack of a stronger national government was very concerning to George Washington.

As former commander in chief of the military, he had witnessed the inherent weakness and inabilities of a government under The Articles of Confederation to recruit and retain soldiers. Washington's fears were nearly realized when a band of Massachusetts farmers, led by Daniel Shays, were on the cusp of waging an armed rebellion against their state's efforts to foreclose on farms to satisfy tax debt. Fortunately for the young nation, Shays Rebellion was put down almost as quickly as it began. This incident, however, worried Washington because he understood how quickly disenfranchised citizens in other states would try and duplicate the efforts of a successful uprising, and because the United States had no national government to speak of, it could be disastrous for the nation.

In true Washingtonian form, the former general decided to act, and he began to correspond with James Madison and others about the need to reform the government. Washington saw his opportunity to act when he served as the head of a commission to build canals that would connect the Potomac and Ohio rivers. Washington invited the commission to Mount Vernon, where he used the opportunity to talk about the tremendous efforts it would take to get all states in agreement on the proposed waterways since there was no strong national government. The commission sent requests for a meeting of the four states which would be affected by the canals (including Virginia). In the Virginia legislature, James Madison recommended that all states be invited to the meeting. Although all states were invited to the commission meeting, only five states attended, but Madison and Washington used the opportunity to facilitate a discussion about the poor state of the economy and the need to revisit and possibly revise The Articles of Confederation. It was here at this meeting that both James Madison and Alexander Hamilton proposed a convention of states, which quickly became a Constitutional Convention.

When the convention convened, the first order of business was to select a presiding officer. When the nominations were opened, Robert Morris from Philadelphia nominated George Washington, and with unanimous consent, he was selected. Although the original purpose of the meeting was to revise The Articles of Confederation, it soon became clear that a total makeover was required. On May 29,

1787, Edmund Randolph from Virginia stood and proposed fifteen resolutions, which, together, became known as the Virginia Plan. The Virginia Plan called for a new form of government with three branches: executive, legislative, and judicial. There is little doubt that the Virginia Plan's principal author, James Madison, had developed this proposal in its earliest stages during one of his many stays at Mount Vernon, under the guidance of...you guessed it: George Washington. Although the Virginia Plan was ultimately altered by what became known as the Connecticut Compromise, Washington was satisfied that the inadequacies of The Articles of Confederation had been corrected and work could begin on forming a new constitution that would govern the specific duties and roles of the three branches of government.

Good Sense and Patriotism

As you can imagine, the convention delegates debated furiously over the details and, at one point in July, reached a complete impasse. The issue which almost wrecked the convention was whether the second chamber of the legislative branch (the Senate) would be composed of an equal number of representatives from each state or, like the first chamber (House of Representatives), have representation based on population. The larger states favored representation based on population, and the smaller states, worried that the larger states would always be able to bully them, favored equal representation. Multiple speeches were made to the delegates, and after two votes, no consensus could be reached.

Charles Pinckney from South Carolina proposed that a committee be formed with one delegate from each state to work on the issue and come back with a recommendation. When the convention reconvened after a two-day recess, the committee recommended that the House of Representatives would be chosen by popular election and representation based on a state's population while the Senate would be composed of two representatives from each state, chosen by that state's legislature. When the convention voted on the matter, the compromise won by one vote. No one was entirely happy with the compromise, including Washington, who wrote, "To please all is impossible, and to attempt it would be vain. The only way, therefore, is to form such a government as will bear the scrutinizing eye of criticism, and trust it to the good sense and patriotism of the people to carry it into effect."[24]

I don't want you to miss that. Go back and read the quote from Washington again. Did you see what he did? He understood that he and his generation were going to do everything in their power and wisdom to create a nation and government that fairly reflected their vision for the republic, and after that, the only thing he could do was rely on us to have "the good sense and patriotism" to keep it. If George Washington was anything, he was a man of action. He didn't hesitate when it came time for war, and he didn't hesitate when he realized that The Articles of Confederation were ineffective. However, he also knew that a day would come when his generation would pass and, in a stunning display of optimism, placed his hope in us. In this instance, his action was to place his hope in future Americans. That means that, for the republic to thrive, future generations must exhibit both good sense *and* patriotism. That's a tall order.

I don't want us to gloss over what Washington meant by "good sense and patriotism." Without reading too much into it, I think it's fair to say that, by "good sense," he means that future generations will approach the business of the nation with reasonable and intelligent thought, with an eye on the past to stay grounded, and the other eye on the future so that whatever we eventually become will be grounded in who the Founding Fathers meant for us to be. "Good sense" doesn't imply ridiculously high IQs or law degrees. It also doesn't imply that the only ones capable of keeping our nation on the right path are lifetime politicians or embedded bureaucrats. What it does imply is that Americans won't make decisions that go against our historic values or that violate our own self-interests.

Trivia question: have Americans ever made decisions that violate our own historical values? Answer: absolutely. Does anyone remember reading about the Trail of Tears? What about succession,

---

[24] https://lehrmaninstitute.org/history/constitution-revised.html

slavery, and the Civil War? Who thinks Jim Crow laws were reflective of the values of George Washington, John Adams, James Madison, or Alexander Hamilton? Tell me why it took so long for women to receive the right to vote, or why Native Americans weren't considered citizens until 1924? You know…the people that were here when Europeans arrived? We definitely have a lot to be ashamed of. We've done things as a nation that are embarrassing and cruel, however, these things alone are not what define us.

We've displayed "good sense" on more than one occasion, and the European continent would be a fascist oasis if Americans had not gotten involved…twice. What about charity? Americans are the most charitable people on earth to the tune of over $400 billion dollars donated per year, and that doesn't include Federal funds that are used to assist needy nations. When it comes to keeping the world healthy, it is the United States that leads the way. Nearly sixty percent of newly developed therapies available globally are funded by United States pharmaceutical companies. Our form of government and economic philosophy has made it possible for the world to live longer and healthier than any other time in human history.

Washington also said that we must be patriots if we want our republic to last. His meaning is clear: patriots love their country. He knew that it didn't matter how much "good sense" future Americans displayed if they didn't love their country. Unfortunately, we only have one word in English for "love," even though it clearly has many different meanings. For instance, I love my wife, and I also love my kids, but it's not the same. I also love Mexican food, deer hunting, and University of Georgia football, but, again, not in the same way. I also love my country, but that love is different than my love for my wife, kids, or Mexican food. What, then, did Washington mean by patriotism? Am I supposed to love my country more or less than Mexican food? Probably more, but the best answer is that you should love it differently.

Patriotism isn't blind love or ill-conceived devotion. Patriotism is affection and loyalty for your country with an understanding that, although imperfect, it is both yours and your offspring's homeland, but it's more than that. A patriot stands ready to serve her country and defend it against domestic or foreign enemies that pose physical threats as well as against ideals that are opposed to the ideals that have historically defined that nation. To be sure, patriotism can be misplaced, and we've seen evil deeds perpetuated in the name of patriotism, but the case against patriotism shouldn't be made based on the actions of fringe groups. Rather, American patriotism is rooted in the ideals expressed in the Declaration of Independence and codified in the United States Constitution, and a patriot, at least as far as Washington was concerned, has great affection and is willing to take action on behalf of both.

Finding Washington

I guess my dad was both right and wrong. When it comes to planning for retirement, hope isn't a strategy. In this regard, he was right as rain. When it comes to preserving a republic and the ideals that formed it, hope is the last leg of a long-term strategy of each generation as we do all we can, and then hope our kids pick up the mantle and preserve our values. Generally speaking, I'd say that Americans have done a decent job at preserving the values espoused in the Declaration of Independence, but I'm also afraid that my generation is purposefully trying to redefine and reimage what it means to be American. It appears genuine disdain for this country earns you more credibility in certain circles than professing affection for it.

To be clear, I think it is possible to love the United States without ignoring the stupidity of previous generations. I can say that I love this country without agreeing with or justifying what happened when President Roosevelt and his administration doubled down on prejudice against Blacks through redlining. If you don't know what that is, look it up. I love the United States, but I don't love the Vietnam War. I don't love the Mexican American War either. I don't love the way we've treated Native Americans, Blacks, women, or other minorities, including Irish immigrants, and I especially don't love that we've assassinated four of our presidents. But those acts don't define us any more than your alcoholic uncle defines your entire family.

I think we must do a better job of preparing the next generation to take over when we're gone. The America we are leaving them is divided in every way imaginable. We're so stupid that we've managed to politicize a pandemic. Think about that for a moment. We have elected leaders in this country that said Covid-19 was not transmissible if you protest, but it was if you went to church. Maybe they didn't use that exact language, but they were absolutely saying this through their actions. We've reached a point where we refuse to acknowledge when someone of a different political ideology than us does something good. In fact, if our party's president does something that we think is good, we're willing to say that the exact same actions by a president of another party is evil. The proud manner in which we display our stupidity is overwhelming.

And do you know who has the most to gain from our divisiveness (besides our enemies)? The free press. Let's face it—good news doesn't sell. Newspapers don't put "Timmy saves his dog from a fire" above the fold. Fox News doesn't scroll "Paul and Anna reconcile their marriage" across the bottom of the screen. Why? Because these companies aren't in the business of making us feel safe. They're in the business of selling fear so that you'll keep reading and tuning in. Listen, if you're in the newspaper or cable news industry, I know that's offensive, and you may not personally feel this way, but generally speaking, this is how the news has always gotten peddled in this country. The difference between us and previous generations is that they didn't have twenty-four-hour news channels or instant, real-time access to information via the internet. I'm telling you that we have to change this, or the next generation is going to be so embroiled in and immobilized by fear that they are going to willingly abdicate their freedoms in exchange for perceived safety.

We need to give our children hope. We need to learn to disagree without hate, and we need to, as a nation, free ourselves from the negative divisiveness that comes our way through the news media and social media. In fact, I think each of us should gather our families together tonight and come up with a plan to abstain from news media and social media for thirty days and then implement a real-life, practical plan for limited engagement moving forward. Look, I get it. You're addicted to your iPhone as much as your kids are. It's your heroin. I'm not saying that it will be easy, but it's been my experience that the right thing is always harder to do than the wrong thing.

The other thing we must do is teach our kids that we don't hate people with differing political ideals. Around the Raines home, we reserve our hate for rival football teams, not political parties. Do me a favor. While you're having your family meeting about abstaining from news and social media, end your meeting by praying for three people in the other political party that you can't stand. If you're a Democrat, pray for President Trump, Mitch McConnell, and Ben Shapiro. If you're a Republican, pray for President Obama, Chuck Schumer, and Rachel Maddow. Pray for God's blessings on their family. Pray for protection and wisdom for these people, and pray like you mean it because God can detect sarcasm and insincerity. Do it so that your kids will see that you have hope, even if you are personally struggling with hope. If we are diligent, then we can display Washington's "good sense and patriotism" in a way that preserves our ideals for one more generation and then hope they preserve it for the generation to come.

CHAPTER 12

Conclusion

Any Last Words?

My dad loved Westerns, and he passed that love onto me. I've been a fan of Clint Eastwood longer than I've been a fan of any other actor. I've seen all his movies (including *Any Which Way But Loose*), especially his Westerns. One of my all-time favorite movies is *The Outlaw Josie Wales*, and if you haven't seen it, you need to stop reading and watch it. I mean, I'd love for my book to be so riveting that you can't put it down, but Josie Wales is the real deal!

One of my other favorite Eastwood movies is *Hang 'Em High*. In this movie, Eastwood is wrongfully accused of a crime and is hung by the bad guy, only to be discovered by a passing lawman and saved. The rest of the movie is about Eastwood's character hunting down the bad guy and bringing him to justice. There's a scene in the movie where a group of men are about to be executed by hanging and are offered the chance to say any last words. One of the condemned gives a lengthy speech about all the actions that led him to the hangman's noose. One of the other condemned prisoners says that his last words are a request that the other man stop talking so they can get it over with. Well, that's what this chapter is. It's my final words to you. I feel like we've gotten to know one another pretty well, and I'm going to miss the time we've spent together, but I've reached a point where I've said my peace, and I need to leave you with some parting thoughts.

What about Jesus?

I have great respect and admiration for George Washington. Like no other during his time, he was the most essential American. I've tried to communicate his importance to the formation of our nation and, along the way, identify various virtues that he displayed which we desperately need to rediscover as a nation. During the initial process of writing this book, I allowed a select group of people to read it so I could get instant feedback. Many of the things you've read in this book are a result of that feedback. One of the questions I've gotten along the way is why I identified George Washington's virtues as the thing we need to rediscover and not a revival of the Christian faith. That's a fair question. I am a Christian and have dedicated my life to the pursuit of higher theological training. I've been active my entire adult life as an integral member of my church as a teacher of Christian theology and am responsible for teaching courses in theology, the history of Christianity, and world religions to college students. It is important that I be as clear as possible here: I believe that the ultimate answer for humanity's problems is found in the person and work of Jesus of Nazareth. It is my desire that every person on the planet discover that.

However, from a historical perspective, this nation has not been a theocracy. We are a republic built on Judeo-Christian principles. Most of our Founding Fathers were Christians, but not all of them. For instance, Thomas Paine and Thomas Jefferson were deists and were generally dissatisfied with the Christian church as an organization. Even so, they believed in the ethics and morality taught in the Jewish and Christian scriptures, which are also reflected in the virtues I have highlighted here that Washington possessed. It is important that you, the reader (particularly the Christian reader) understand that I am not substituting Washington's virtues for the freedom that Jesus brings. I am, however, saying that, regardless of our faith traditions, we need to participate in a revival of Washington's virtues before we lose our country. That means that anyone of most any faith tradition, particularly the world's most predominant religions (Hinduism, Buddhism, Daoism, Indigenous worship, and the three

Abrahamic religions), should find themes that are compatible with their faith. It is unlikely that you will find a religious person that thinks we need less integrity and empathy in our culture.

What's Next?

I've always been fascinated with why people choose to write books. At the very least, you have to consider that narcissism is an underlying factor. You must be a little narcissistic to think others would want to read something you've written. One of my favorite stories about why a person decided to write a book is also a sad story. When General Ulysses S. Grant decided to resign from the army and run for president, he forfeited his army pension in the process. In those days, there was no pension for former presidents, which meant that, after his presidency, he had to rely on previous investments or savings to survive. Unfortunately, he was the victim of theft by a crooked investor, and upon learning he had tongue cancer, he realized he had no money to care for his family once he was gone. To remedy his financial woes, former President Grant offered to write an autobiography, which Mark Twain agreed to publish. Grant's autobiography is still heralded as the best autobiography of any former United States president and is still in print. Grant finished his book and then died a few days later. His widow received over $400,000 in royalties from the book, which more than provided for her needs after he was gone.[25]

It's sad that Grant died before he could see the positive impacts of his efforts on his family and the preservation of history. Others write because they enjoy research and the creative process, and others write because they're good at it. I have to be honest with you. I wrote this book for an entirely different reason. First, I'm certainly a bit of a narcissist, but that's not the only reason. Secondly, I'm not doing it for the money because, honestly, I don't even know how much you

---

[25] To hear all the specifics, I recommend that you listen to the "Presidential" podcast by Washington Post reporter Lillian Cunningham and, for the purposes of this illustration, the episode on President Ulysses S. Grant.

get paid for writing a book. You may find this odd, but my reason for writing is two-fold.

First, I really do love this country. Unless you define patriotism as what the Timothy McVeigh's of the world do, I'm certainly a patriot. When I look around, I see that we are in danger of losing our republic from within. Our greatest enemy hasn't been other nations. It has always been our willingness to let things divide us. You may think I'm an alarmist and I've lost my mind, but from a historical perspective, we are almost as divided today as we were prior to the Civil War, except this time, the division can't be defined according to state lines. This book is my way of trying to convince us to use Washington as an example for how to be good citizens and neighbors. Secondly, and you're going to laugh, I sense that writing this book is part of God's divine purpose for my life, even if the only ones that read it are my kids.

So what do we do now? The last thing I want is for you to finish this book and simply move on with your life. That would be a waste of both of our time. I desperately want to engage you, the reader, in a way that perhaps an author has never engaged his or her reader. I've given you my email in previous chapters, but just in case you missed it, here it is again: richard@findingwashington.com. I want to hear from you about how you are teaching the contents of this book to your kids. I want to hear how you are working to personally adopt some of Washington's virtues. I want you to share stories from Washington's life that highlight virtues I haven't talked about. I desperately want to hear how you are shunning the social narrative that we are an evil country, and I want to hear how you have become an ambassador for hope to the next generation. I want you to start a book club and invite me to a Zoom meeting so I can hear what you have to say. And if you think I won't join you for a Zoom, you're out of your mind. As far as I'm concerned, the worst thing that could happen is for me to write this book and then never know if it made any difference. So the answer to the question, "What's next" is that you become the Mom, Dad, citizen, and neighbor that George Washington would be proud of.

Finding Washington

There is one more story from Washington's life that I want to leave with you. As we all know, once the Constitution and Bill of Rights were ratified, the people elected Washington to serve as the nation's first president. After two terms, he left public life and headed back to his beloved Mount Vernon and returned to farming. Both George and Martha's letters during this time reveal that they were, perhaps, the happiest they had ever been. The president wrote that he would begin his day at dawn and not return until dinner, where he and Martha would usually entertain guests. His only regret during this time is that he had difficulty finding time to read. Although he was content to be out of the public eye, he still corresponded with friends about the issues of the day, and he was particularly concerned with political partisanship and how easily Americans would align themselves with various ideologies and argue among themselves (sound familiar?). In 1797, he wrote to his friend William Heath and expressed his frustration about how he wished Americans would stop siding with either England or France and simply focus on being Americans.

In 1798, President John Adams was struggling with how to deal with increasingly hostile actions from the French and, in response, approved the formation of a standing army. Reluctantly, the former general said goodbye once more to Martha and Mount Vernon and, with Alexander Hamilton at his side, presided over the formation and training of a new American fighting force. His reason?

> "As my whole life has been dedicated to my country, in shape or another, for the poor remains of it, it is not an object to contend for ease and quiet, when all that is valuable in it is at stake, further than to be satisfied that the sacrifice I should make of them is acceptable and desired by my country. The principles by which my conduct has been actuated through life would not suffer me, in any great emergency, to withhold

any services I could render required by my country; especially in a case where its dearest rights are assailed by lawless ambition and intoxicated power, contrary to every principle of justice, and in violation of solemn compacts and laws, which govern all civilized nations...In circumstances like these, accompanied by an actual invasion of our territorial rights, it would be difficult at any time for me to remain an idle spectator under the plea of age and retirement."[26]

If Washington's use of the English language makes it difficult for you to interpret what he's saying, let me sum it up for you. He is saying that he has dedicated his entire life to principles that make it impossible for him to withhold service to his country, and age or retirement is no excuse. Even in the twilight of his life, our most essential Founding Father refused to say no to his country in a time of need. He understood that, to preserve the republic and its principles, good people could not stop fighting, even when we have a good excuse like old age or retirement.

There is no room here for parsing terms or making light of our current situation. We live in an era where people of influence and some of those that serve in our government hate this country. When they read our history, all they see are the mistakes and not the mountain of examples where the United States was, and still is, a beacon of hope for the world. We live in an age where those that hate America do not desire civil debate. Rather, they are, like all fascists, dictators, and purveyors of dissent, authoritarians that want to destroy anyone that disobeys their demands to deconstruct our society and the values upon which our nation was formed. They applaud mob rule and chaos while vilifying justice. Like it or not, this is our generation's fight, and, like Washington, we must not offer excuses as to why we are silent.

---

[26] Benson J. Lossing, *Washington and the American Republic* (Virtue and Yorston: New York, 1879), 511–512.

Likewise, our society is obsessed with sensuality and vulgarity. Through technology, our children are exposed to things that previous generations only whispered about, or men made jokes about but had never actually seen. It is a disservice to our children that, before they are old enough to engage in sexual activity, they have, most likely, seen hundreds of sexual acts through free access to internet pornography. We are just now beginning to see the adverse effects that unlimited access to pornography is having on our culture. Depression and body dysmorphic disorder are real problems in both male and female teenagers. Children are engaging in sexual activity younger than previous generations, and if you don't think that's a problem, then you are part of the problem. And while our children are watching pornography, the rest of us have our face buried in an electronic device obsessed with social media or entertainment. At what point do we say "enough is enough" and revive the virtues that are absent from our culture?

I could go on with more examples, but I don't want my last words to you to be negative. I merely want you to see the urgency of my premise, which is the need for a revival of virtues like the ones George Washington displayed. We need leaders with integrity, empathy, and compassion, who display good character and conviction, who aren't afraid to fail or change their views if they realize those views are wrong, and who are genuine in their conduct. We've spent twelve chapters trying to *find Washington*, and if you're still reading, then you are the Washington I so desperately wanted to find.

I wish had more time with you, and I wish I had more solutions. I am, however, comforted knowing that the brilliance and ingenuity that is uniquely American will reveal itself as you lead your family and community. It's not going to be easy. Doing the right thing seldom is, but it will be worth it. It will be worth it when our efforts bring about a change in how we discuss politics. It will be worth it when our kids aren't growing up too fast, and it will be worth it when everyone isn't angry all the time. It will be worth it when we aren't obsessed with social media or only posting our highlight reels, and it will certainly be worth it when we can look up to our leaders again.

We have work to do. Let's get to it. I can't wait to hear from you.

Postscript

Almost an entire year has passed since I wrote the last sentence of the previous chapter and, boy, are things tenuous in our country. In 2020, masks were the ultimate status symbol, but masks have been replaced with the vaccine. I don't want to misrepresent the current reality, but let me try and explain it. Proponents of the Covid vaccine want everyone to be vaccinated because the vaccine offers the best protection against the virus. I generally agree with this, and my entire family was vaccinated. However, many proponents of the vaccine are super-duper angry at the unvaccinated because they think unvaccinated people pose a risk to vaccinated people. So the message is "Get the vaccine so you won't get Covid." But the message is also "Get the vaccine so you won't give Covid to the vaccinated." But the message is also "Immigrants pouring across the border do not have to be vaccinated because (checks liberal media talking points) racism." And people are really, really, mad about all of this.

We're also watching our president deteriorate physically on national television, and it ain't pretty. My heart breaks for him, and Jessica and I pray for him often. We're also still dealing with a struggling economy with no significant sign of relief. Oh, did I mention that former President Trump has been banned from Twitter and Facebook but the Taliban haven't? Speaking of the Taliban, they are now 2-0 against world superpowers, so there's that.

I'm not going to drone on and on about the state of things. You watch the news and know that things are devolving rapidly. The point of this chapter is not to talk more about Washington and his virtues or what's happening in the news. It's to talk about you. Yes, you.

I hope you realize that nothing is going to change unless you, as an individual, commit to living a life defined by positive moral virtues. I know that it feels like we're outnumbered, but you're wrong. There are more of us. We are in the majority, and the lying liars from Liar Town who mandate that we live by a set of rules that do not apply to them are in the minority. The reason you think we're in the minority is because the idiots have the microphone, and they spend all day screaming from cable news studios and social media platforms that you're a racist/bigot/homophobe if you want to see a return of traditional moral values. It's going to be hard, but you have to stop listening to them. It's imperative that you turn off cable news and stop looking at social media every 2.5 seconds. It's killing our country.

I want you to know that I'm rooting for you. I've given you my email several times, and I couldn't be more serious about staying in touch with you. I look forward to hearing from you soon.

Richard(richard@findingwashington.com)

About the Author

When asked about the kind of impact Richard Raines has made on those around him, the reviews speak for themselves. The Raines family dog, Cody, enthusiastically said, "The human sometimes feeds me when the teenagers don't."

When his kids were asked to comment on what it was like having a parent that is also a writer, his seventeen-year-old son affectionately said, "He wrote a book?"

And his fifteen-year-old son characteristically said, "Huh?"

The other children were adamant in their praise that "Yes, he is our dad."

His wife, Jessica, lovingly said, "I haven't read it yet but feel like I have because he won't stop talking about it."

When Richard isn't using humor and sarcasm to communicate, he can be found living, worshipping, serving, working, teaching, and writing from his home in Northeast Florida. Richard earned his undergraduate degree from Lee University, two graduate degrees from Regent University, and is pursuing his PhD from Midwestern Baptist Theological Seminary. Originally from South Georgia, he enjoys hunting, fishing, and Georgia Bulldog football.

CPSIA information can be obtained
at www.ICGtesting.com
Printed in the USA
BVHW040349010622
638444BV00025B/70